Looking for Love
in All the
Wrong Places

Also by Jed Diamond, L.C.S.W.

Inside Out: Becoming My Own Man

LOOKING FOR LOVE IN ALL THE WRONG PLACES

OVERCOMING ROMANTIC AND SEXUAL ADDICTIONS

Jed Diamond, L.C.S.W.

G. P. PUTNAM'S SONS   New York

G. P. Putnam's Sons
Publishers Since 1838
200 Madison Avenue
New York, NY 10016

Library of Congress Cataloging-in-Publication Data

Diamond, Jed, date
  Looking for love in all the wrong places.

  Bibliography: p.
  Includes index.
  1. Love. 2. Intimacy (Psychology) 3. Attachment behavior.
I. Title.
HQ801.D53   1988   306.7   88-4235
ISBN 0-399-13372-0

Printed in the United States of America
1   2   3   4   5   6   7   8   9   10

Acknowledgments

I would like to thank the following people who helped bring this book to life:

My wife, Carlin, and my children—Aaron, Angela, and Jemal; my mother, Edith Diamond, and my father, Morris Diamond; Sally Dennett, my research associate; my editor at Putnam's, Lisa Wager, and the other staff at Putnam's, including C. J. Hall, Marilyn Ducksworth, and Lisa Johnson; Clyde Taylor, my agent, and the staff of Curtis Brown Ltd.

And my heartfelt appreciation to the many clients who have had the courage to confront and overcome their own romantic and sexual addictions.

This book is dedicated to the people in the Anonymous programs who support each other in recovery and those professionals who have had the courage to confront their own addictions.

CONTENTS

PART III   GETTING FREE

Author's Note

Addictions are as old as humankind, yet the ability to treat them is new. We are still discovering how to overcome romantic and sexual addictions, but we can't afford to wait until all the information is in before we make it available. This book offers my own insights as a therapist, gathered over the past twenty-five years, as well as my personal experience as a recovering love addict. In it I use the terms "love addiction," "romantic and sexual addictions," and "sex and love addiction" interchangeably and somewhat loosely, since the book is meant as an overview of a new and complex field of treatment and is therefore more general than precise.

Looking for Love in All the Wrong Places is primarily for people who are concerned about their romantic relationships, but I believe it will also be of interest to counselors, clinicians, other professionals, and those in academia. Much of what I say about romantic addiction, addictions generally, the relationship between addictions and society, and the treatment of addictions is different from what many are used to hearing. I trust the ideas will stimulate your thinking, your own research, and help us all to deal more effectively with our own dependencies and be more effective in our role as helpers.

Jed Diamond, L.C.S.W.

INTRODUCTION

When we find that our romantic relationships are a series of disappointments yet continue to pursue them, we are looking for love in all the wrong places. When we are overwhelmed by our physical attraction to a new person, when the chemistry feels "fantastic," and we are sure that *this* time we have found someone who will make us whole, we are looking for love in all the wrong places. When we are in a committed relationship but find ourselves constantly attracted to others, we are looking for love in all the wrong places. When *our* desire for "more sex" interferes with our family or professional lives, we are looking for love in all the wrong places. When we are as preoccupied with not having sex as others are with having it, we are looking for love in all the wrong places.

Many of us are unhappy with our romantic relationships but don't know what to do about it. There are times we swear "never again." Getting close is just too painful. But there is only so much energy we can devote to our jobs, our friends, our hobbies. Sooner or later we return to the search for love. We become hooked on destructive relationships that we can't leave, and hooked on an endless search for romantic intrigue. Whether swearing off men or

13

women, or actively pursuing them, we eventually become obsessed. We can't live with them and we can't live without them. We ride a roller coaster of hope and despair.

When we look around at friends and family, read the newspapers, glance through magazines, or watch television, it seems that everyone is "doing it"—but few people are truly satisfied with their romantic lives. Until recently love addiction has been hidden. Now we are beginning to learn more about romantic involvements that have gotten out of control, especially as they touch the lives of the rich and famous. First we learned about Jim Bakker's involvement with Jessica Hahn and then Gary Hart's affair with Donna Rice. We saw the movie *Fatal Attraction* and found out that love addiction is deadly.

Attachment and Attraction

Much has been written recently about ways in which people become dependent on relationships that are destructive, about "women who love too much" and "men who hate women." People who seem unable to leave relationships that are unhealthy are hooked on a need for *attachment*. But there is another side to the coin: For every person who is hooked on attachment, there is a person who can't seem to commit to just one relationship. This person is always looking for a partner. For this person sex and romantic intrigue become the fuel that drive them. These people are hooked on *attraction*.

For those people who are dependent on attachment to another person, the primary need is for *connection*. Their irrational fear is of *loss* or *abandonment*. By contrast, those who are dependent on their attraction to multiple partners have a primary need for *space*. Their irrational fear is of being *bound* or *trapped*.

Although we might conclude that people hooked on attraction are totally different from those hooked on attachment, they are actually quite closely related. For one thing, they often become hooked on each other. People who "can't let go" find people who "can't say no" very attractive. People hooked on avoiding commitment become very dependent when the relationship seems in

14

danger. People who may have been totally dependent on a partner at one time in their lives may find at other times that they lust after many different people and can't settle down with one person. Those hooked on attraction often seem to have difficulty in the sexual area, while those hooked on attachment often have difficulty with intimacy. Yet I believe that all these seeming differences between them are merely different aspects of the same underlying problem.

In this book we will take a hard look at the reasons so many of us, looking for someone to love, seem inevitably to find relationships that are unsatisfying and unhealthy. And we will explore why we continue to re-create relationships that don't work. We will see that looking for love while we still feel like frightened, insecure children inside becomes a futile search. We will come to understand that looking for love in all the wrong places turns the search for romantic fulfillment into an addiction.

The Hidden Addiction

Dr. Stanton Peele, an authority on addictions, says, "Many of us are addicts, only we don't know it. We turn to each other out of the same needs that drive some people to drink and others to heroin. Interpersonal addiction—love addiction—is just about the most common yet least recognized form of addiction we know."[1]

We might ask why we have never heard of this form of addiction. I believe it is because we live in a culture where love addiction is so common that it's become invisible.

Many of the beliefs we learned as children were reinforced by the culture as we grew up. Although the sexual revolution of the 60's and 70's helped many to overcome sexual dysfunction and to accept sex as a normal part of human life, it also had a dark side that has received little attention. As birth-control pills became more widely available, women gained control over their bodies. As sex researchers taught us more about the physiology of orgasm, we learned to have greater control over our sexual pleasure. We learned that premature ejaculation, impotence, inability to achieve orgasm, and pain during intercourse could be treated.

15

The sexual revolution promised a golden age of sexual freedom and responsiveness. We would all be granted the sexual pleasure and enjoyment that was our birthright. In our commitment to make love, not war, we would bring about a new world based on freedom, equality, and sensual delight.

At least that was the dream. What went wrong? Our newly discovered knowledge and technology was supposed to produce the pleasures of sexual freedom. Instead we seem to have produced the horrors of sexual compulsion.

Let's take another look at the sexual revolution to discover what we missed. It did indeed offer us greater options for living, but it also had another aspect that slid by unnoticed. In separating sexual intercourse from "procreation," we also separated sex from "creation."

We truly need to limit the number of children we bring into the world. But we cannot afford to limit the amount of creation and love. When sex became separated from creation, we stopped making love and started "scoring." We lost our ability to connect with the sacred in life. We became strangers to the "I-thou" relationship and got hooked on the "I-it."

We forgot that the originators of the Judeo-Christian tradition did not speak of the engaging, pleasuring, person-integrating, total relationship between a man and a woman as "making babies," "making love," or "getting it on." Instead they used the simple rich word *yahdah*, "knowing." The sexual revolution was supposed to create an environment in which men and women could relate as sexual equals. Instead it produced men and women who hardly know each other.

In order to overcome an addiction, we must first be aware that it exists. This book chronicles the addictive search for love.

The word *addiction* is frightening, conjuring up images of the Man with the Golden Arm shooting heroin into his veins. It makes us think of movie stars and sports heroes who have killed themselves with cocaine. We picture alcoholics begging for a quarter to get some "food." Yet addictions are much more inclusive than these stereotypes suggest. According to the Oxford English Dictionary, addiction was originally a term in Roman law meaning "a surrender, or dedication, of anyone to a master." It is in this broader sense of losing control and becoming unhealthily dependent on another person that I use the word addiction in this book.

But many will still have a difficult time conceiving of romance and sex as things we could get "hooked" on. And even if we could get hooked, who would mind? That's one addiction we'd love to have! We agree, as a culture, with the wisdom of Hollywood: You can't ever be too rich or too thin. And you can't ever have too much romance and sex.

Slowly, we are beginning to question Tinseltown ideals. When we see pictures of a reclusive Howard Hughes living out his days in fear, afraid to touch anything for fear of picking up germs, we wonder what happiness all his money brought him. When we learn that cute, lithe Karen Carpenter died of anorexia, we think twice about the value of thinness.

Yet it isn't alcohol, drugs, money, thinness, sex or romance that are the real problems, but rather what we are willing to sacrifice of ourselves in order to have them. In our endless search for the magic "fix," we gradually lose our connection to our very being.

Too many of us have traded the beauty of our real selves for the fool's gold of romantic intrigue. In spite of the cultural belief that love addicts don't exist, they can be found everywhere:

- The woman who is so fearful of sex she becomes obsessed with killing off her sexual desire and starves herself much as an anorexic starves herself of food;
- The man who can't stop having affairs even though he has lost interest in them and they threaten the stability of his family life;
- The woman, three years in recovery from alcoholism, who finds that her sexual preoccupation with older men has made her life miserable and threatens her sobriety;
- The anti-pornography activist who is obsessed with stamping out sex and whose own sexual behavior becomes increasingly compulsive and destructive to his own peace and well-being;

17

- The bisexual man who continues to have multiple sexual encounters in spite of the fact that he knows he is subjecting himself and his wife to the likelihood of AIDS;
- The successful female executive who cruises waterfront bars and picks up men who are dangerous;
- The author of this book, a successful psychotherapist, husband, and father of three teenage children . . .

I thought I could make up for what I had missed in childhood by finding the "great love" of my life. I married a woman who, like myself, had lost her father early in life. I clung to her in spite of our numerous problems. I became an "attachment junkie." I couldn't seem to let go no matter how bad things became. When we finally did break up, I went through an addict's withdrawal. I couldn't sleep. I ate constantly. I thought often of suicide.

Then I went to the other extreme and became an "attraction junkie." I drowned my misery in a long series of sexual encounters. I couldn't keep my eyes off beautiful bodies. I was like a kid in a candy store. I wanted one of everything and I wanted as much as I could get, as fast as I could get it. Most of the time, I wasn't even sure what I wanted, but it seemed absolutely vital that I have it.

I "fell in love" and had an affair with the wife of a security guard who repaired guns in his spare time. I knew I was in trouble when I found myself justifying the deadly situation I had created. What the hell, I thought. We all have to die sometime. This wouldn't be a half-bad way to go.

Needless to say, I didn't find love, but I couldn't stop looking. The pattern repeated itself many times before I concluded that something was wrong. As a trained psychotherapist, I couldn't understand how I could help so many others find happiness without being able to find it myself.

A 12-Step Approach

I had always been attracted to working with alcoholics and drug addicts. I didn't have any addictions myself, I felt, but for some reason I was comfortable working with their addictions. I began going to a number of self-help groups such as Synanon and Alcoholics Anonymous so that I would have a better understanding of how to help my clients.

As I listened to the stories of lost dreams, compulsive chemical use, and destructive behavior, something rang a bell in me. I thought, Maybe I'm an alcoholic but don't know it. Gradually I realized that if I substituted romantic and sexual addictions for alcoholism, the problem was the same.

In those days no one thought love relationships could be addictive. So I kept my idea to myself. But to my amazement, as I adapted AA, Al-Anon, and other 12-step programs to my own situation, things began to improve in my life.

My initial fear about going to meetings and trying to follow the steps was that I would have to give up making love. After all, I'd heard that the only cure for addictions is abstinence. You don't get well until you "put the plug in the jug." But I learned that there *are* important differences as well as similarities between chemical addictions and love addictions. I breathed a sigh of relief when I learned the most basic difference is that we don't need to give up love and sex to recover from our addiction to unhealthy relationships.

If this is a concern of yours, let me reassure you: I won't be asking you to give up love or sex, any more than I would ask someone with an eating disorder to give up food. I won't even be asking you to change anything about your romantic or sexual behavior, *unless and until you are ready*. It is possible that you may not even have to change anything: Sometimes just having an awareness of the situation you are in, its cause and effect, is sufficient to turn it around.

I've learned that our addictions have a positive side as well as a negative one. They are old and trusted friends. They were there for us when no one else was. They were even necessary for our survival. The thought of giving up our addictions has all the appeal of giving up our best friend, our right arm, or life itself. They may seem to be causing us problems now, but they also give us great comfort.

19

In this book you will find no demands or even suggestions to give up your addiction. I am going to offer you a way of "getting more" of something rather than "giving up" something—more safety and security in your life. This book will help you feel better about yourself and those around you. It will show you the right places to look for love. And, it will teach you how to have all the love that you so richly deserve in your life. As you feel more secure and cared for, old, unhealthy ways of being will disappear from your life.

The Journey to Health

Let me give you a preview of what you will find in *Looking for Love in All the Wrong Places*. The book is divided into three sections. In the first, we will explore the nature of romantic and sexual addictions. You will meet the wide range of people who are in addictive relationships. You will learn the behaviors that constitute love addiction and the ways these behaviors interfere with our lives. If you are concerned that someone you care about may be addicted to romance or sex, you will be able to gain a deeper understanding of the addictive process. You will get a first-hand glimpse into addicted men and their female companions. You will learn about the female addict and her male spouse or lover. Finally, you will see that you are not alone in experiencing the pain of addiction. Dr. Patrick J. Carnes, an expert on sexual addiction, estimates that 1 person in 12 is addicted to sex.[2] Many more are addicted to romance.

The second section will focus on how people become addicted. You will learn that the core of the addictive desire is a need for safety and security that was lacking in early life. You will come to understand the need that love addicts have to control their intimate relationships. You will see how our adult love lives actually re-create the same atmosphere that was present between our mothers and fathers.

In the third section you will learn that love addiction is a problem that *can* be treated successfully. You will learn about the latest research from the fields of chemical dependency, sexology, family

20

therapy, and psychotherapy and what they can add to the effectiveness of treatment. You will learn how successful treatment approaches for alcoholics and drug addicts can be modified and applied to love addiction. You will be given a step-by-step program developed by the author that has worked for over 10,000 people over the past twenty-five years.

You will learn about ways of engaging in romantic relationships that bring about joy and peace rather than pain and fear, and how to develop intimate relationships that are satisfying and long-lasting.

At the end of this book is a self-help questionnaire to help you determine whether you suffer from a love addiction.[3] You can take it any time to get a clear picture of where you stand in relationship to significant others. You can also take it to help you get a clearer picture of someone you care about.

Finally, there is a list of resources for getting help if you need it, along with a bibliography for further reading.

I firmly believe you can free yourself from sexual thoughts and behaviors that interfere with your life. The only question is how long it will take. Each person has a unique path toward health and a unique timetable for developing healthier attitudes toward love.

Some will read this book from cover to cover, identify with much of it, and use it immediately to recover from addictions. Others will read only a few pages, decide the book isn't for them now, and put it away for later. Still others will get angry at what they read, sure the book doesn't have anything to do with them, and throw it in the corner.

There is no right or wrong way to recover from addiction. Use the book in whatever way serves you. Read it from front to back, back to front, or start in the middle. Let your intuition be your guide. Take what is useful to you and forget about the rest.

I often ask my new clients, "Would you give me twenty-five dollars?" They generally give me a funny look and pull back a little. No one wants to give up something. I then ask, "If I give *you* thirty-five dollars, would you give me twenty-five dollars?" They lean forward a bit. One man said with a cautious grin, "If I could trust it was real, you'd have a deal, and I'd keep coming back for more!"

21

In this book you will find a whole series of offers. Each one will ask you to take a small risk in return for a personal gain. You accepted the first offer when you gave up your time to read this book. If you got back more than you gave, you are ready to continue. But there's no hurry. You can move at your own pace. You are in charge. Give up only what you no longer need. You are on a wondrous path with many new delights along the way. Let this book serve as your guide.

Enjoy the journey!

PART I

The Nature of Romantic and Sexual Addictions

1. VICTIMS OF LOVE:
Walking the Wire of Pain and Desire

"I Think I May Have a Problem"

Roger had seen my card at a conference at which I was speaking. ADDICTIVE RELATIONSHIPS SPECIALIST: ALCOHOL, DRUGS, FOOD, PEOPLE, the card read. He called me to say he was having serious problems with the fourth addiction on my list. We made an appointment for the next day.

He arrived precisely at 9:00 A.M., giving off the air of an important executive on-the-go. He was impeccably dressed in an expensive suit, had stylishly cut graying hair, and came ready to do business. He took charge immediately.

"I'm not sure why I'm here," he said. He looked directly at me and waited. I almost felt he expected *me* to talk. In the pause that ensued I thought of the clients I'd seen over the years, particularly the men. They can't really believe they have a problem and pride themselves on being able to handle whatever life has to offer. They consider people who go to "shrinks" or "groups" weak-willed. When they do go for help, often as a result of some outside pressure, they are sure that whatever the "problem" is can be disposed of quickly. Although they desperately need to reach out for help, their tremendous distrust of people makes them keep the helper at a distance. Roger seemed to fit the pattern.

He finally spoke again. "I think I may have a problem," he said in a voice that sounded firm and strong. "You probably saw me at the conference. I was the guy in front that kept getting up every fifteen or twenty minutes to go outside." I shook my head. "No, I don't think I recall." He seemed a little surprised that his getting up wasn't obvious to everyone. "Well, I had this woman in my van and I had to go out all the time just to see her and, you know, give her a little pat."

"How's that a problem?" I asked. (I've learned over the years never to assume I know how some behavior is perceived as a problem by a client, no matter how obvious it may seem to be so in my opinion. I also never dismiss anything a client says, no matter how "normal" it appears.) "Well, it's like I *have* to see her. If I don't I get very anxious." Roger's businesslike manner was beginning to soften now as he talked about Laura, the girl in the van.

"I've been seeing her for about three years. She's young, and beautiful, and exciting. She's the best thing that ever happened to me," he continued with enthusiasm, then paused and looked away. "But she's ruining my life."

"Oh, how so?" I asked.

Roger breathed a long sigh and went on. "Well, I've been married for fifteen years and have three beautiful kids and one on the way. I'm not really unhappy with my wife. I mean, she does everything for me. She never complains and she's a good mother." He paused and looked up again with a sad, faraway look. "We just don't have a lot in common and our sex life is pretty dull. I used to think she was very accepting. Now I wonder if she isn't just indifferent.

"I met Laura at a party and I fell in love the moment I saw her." His voice began to get higher and he spoke more quickly as he went on. "Even though my wife was at the party, Laura and I snuck out and made love standing up against a tree in the garden. It was the most exciting thing I've ever felt. We began seeing each other every week. It wasn't difficult. My wife didn't question me and I told her I had to stay late for meetings at work.

"But once a week wasn't enough for me. I wanted to see Laura

26

more often." Roger paused and shook his head. "I couldn't believe it. She goes to school full-time, carries 18 credits, and works to support herself and her three-year-old boy, but whenever I wanted to see her she would make herself available. And whatever I wanted to do, and I mean *whatever,* she would always do it and let me know she enjoyed it."

I could well understand why Roger wanted to spend more time with Laura, but I still wondered how he perceived this seemingly wonderful arrangement as a problem.

"Pretty soon I began taking off from work to see her, and that's when the trouble began." I nodded as the picture began to fill out. "I was the vice-president of a large San Francisco brokerage house," he continued as he sat up straighter in his chair. I noticed the past tense. "I began missing more and more time at work and eventually was asked to resign. No one knew the reason for my absences, at least I don't think they did." His brow knit as he looked up to the ceiling, reviewing the past events in his mind. "No, I'm sure no one ever knew, and I easily got another job with a rival firm."

I began to see the pattern in Roger's life—sex getting out of control, a good thing gone bad. "Well, it took six months, but the same thing happened in the new job." He slumped a bit in his chair. His suit looked more rumpled and his eyes looked sad. "This time someone found out. They told my boss, and I think they called my wife. Anyway, Ellen found out.

"I couldn't lie to her." He looked up wistfully and slowly shook his head, his voice rising. "I wish she would have gotten angry and yelled at me, threatened to leave, or something! Instead she wanted to know what she had done wrong. She just sat all curled up, rocking back and forth crying softly.

"I swore I would end the affair. I really meant it." There was a tone of defiance and resolve in his voice. But then it trailed off and he looked down at his hands. "I couldn't do it. I got a new job where I traveled a lot. I thought being away from Laura would break the spell. If I didn't see her, I thought I could forget her." He was silent for a long time.

"What happened?" I asked. He seemed to be reaching the end of the story. As he spoke I could feel the hopelessness and desperation in his voice. "I began taking her with me on business trips. I began charging our expenses on the company business card." He turned pale as he went on. "After a fight we had, I bought her a diamond necklace, and charged that to the business. I could see it coming, but couldn't stop it. I got caught, got fired, and only my agreement to make restitution, and their desire to keep things quiet, kept me from going to jail." He took a deep breath and let it out.

"That's the story. I can't keep losing jobs. Being with Laura is destroying my life and I don't seem to be able to stop it."

Willpower Won't Work

Roger exhibits all three signs of addiction. I call them the 3 C's.[1] First is the *compulsion*. Roger feels driven. He believes he needs to see Laura in order to survive. We see the *loss of control* when Roger talks about trying to limit his contact, but being unable to do so. Finally, there is *continuation* of the addictive behavior in spite of the serious consequences it is causing in his life. Even the loss of his job wasn't enough to make Roger change his addictive sexual behavior.

By the time he'd made the appointment with me it was clear to Roger, as it becomes clear to many alcoholics and food and drug addicts, that trying to use willpower to change the behavior is useless. The problem continues to get worse as a person's life becomes more chaotic and self-destructive.

"He's Driving Me Nuts"

The addictive nature of Carol's love life was more hidden, even though she was a recovering alcoholic. Carol was my client for two years before she ever talked openly about her love life. It didn't seem important initially. She had been referred to me by her Alcoholics Anonymous sponsor because her use of pills was interfering with her ability to stay away from alcohol and her husband was, as she reported, driving her "crazy." Her sponsor, Florence, though ten years younger than Carol, was from the old school of AA: "I help focus on the drinking," she told me in her deep, booming voice. "I don't understand this pill use and if she doesn't love her husband, she should just leave him."

Florence would often call me when she was feeling stuck with a "sponsee" and I would come over for tea and cookies, and see if I had any insights that might help. This time, as I sat at the small table in Florence's kitchen listening to Carol talk about her problems, I suddenly felt I was in the presence of a woman who was tremendously angry and fearful.

Carol was an attractive woman in her late thirties who kept in good shape through running. She spoke rapidly and her brow wrinkled as she tore into her husband, George, a stockbroker to whom she had been married for sixteen years. "He's driving me nuts," she began with a voice that seemed to drip with venom. "He doesn't like me going to AA meetings. He still won't accept that I'm an alcoholic even though I almost drank myself to death. He wants me to stay home and take care of him and always be available for him sexually. Who wouldn't take pills if they had to live with a man like George."

I began to see Carol, once a week, with the understanding that I would work closely with her sponsor as well. We concentrated, initially, on getting her off the pills. Originally prescribed to calm her down, they had actually contributed to her mood swings and often led to bouts of drinking when she was "high."

She didn't want to talk about her romantic concerns, even though they seemed to be a source of great stress to her. I didn't push her and felt that helping her stay clean and sober was my main focus.

But now she sat in my office with the same wild anger I had seen when we had met two years previously, and this time she was obviously ready to talk. "I'm afraid I'm going to do something crazy." Carol looked more frightened than I'd ever seen her. The anger that usually gave her a look of invincibility was gone. "Sex with George is disgusting. He just wants to stick it in, get it over with, and go to sleep." Her voice almost pleaded for an answer. "If I don't get some relief, I'm going to go out and get drunk. At least then I'll feel alive. What can I do?"

We talked now about her relationship with her husband. They had met in high school and married in their early twenties. He was a few years older than Carol and she had admired him for his ambition and drive. "He pursued me with the same dedication and purpose that he did everything else in life. He reminded me a little bit of my father, who was also very tall and handsome, and I was very attracted to him."

She shook her head sadly, then with a touch of anger, as she continued. "The honeymoon was short-lived. Once we settled into our new home, all his energy went into his work. Lovemaking became less and less frequent as the first of our four children arrived. It hasn't gotten any better since."

Like her sponsor, I too wondered why Carol had remained married to George. "When I drank it made things easier. It was the only time I could really enjoy making love. When I got sober I felt like all the fun had gone out of my life. I followed the program and believed that things would get better, but without booze I couldn't enjoy making love. And without making love life has been miserable."

The words seemed to tumble out, almost unbidden, as she continued. "Less than a year after I got sober in AA I had an affair with a man I knew from work. I didn't particularly like him, but the sex was exciting and I felt alive again." I could feel, as she described her affair with Ted, that sex for her was like a drug. It covered her pain and brought her pleasure. It was "magic" and she didn't want to lose it. But lose it she did. "George came by one day and caught us. He threatened to leave me and I was almost glad. At least it would have been over, even though the thought of being alone terrified me. I promised it would never happen again, and George agreed to stay.

"Well, it never did happen again, though I think we both wanted it. We just never had the opportunity." Carol looked down at her hands and there was a long silence. "But I've had other affairs, mostly with married men in AA. I know it's wrong and I feel guilty as hell, but I can't seem to stop."

She began talking more rapidly, as if trying to get it all out at once. "I haven't had a lot of affairs, but I fantasize constantly. I want it all the time. I call a particular man five or six times a day, just to hear his voice, and I'm frantic if he isn't home or doesn't return my call. When he isn't around I have fantasies about other men." She paused and tears began to form. I realized I'd never seen Carol cry. "I even have fantasies about making love to my priest and the thought terrifies me."

From Pleasure to Compulsion

Whatever we may think about the morality of having extramarital affairs, sex with people in our therapy groups, or fantasies about our priests, these behaviors aren't necessarily addictive. The distinguishing quality in love addiction is the frightening loss of control.

What begins as a desire for pleasure becomes a painful compulsion. Once we were the engineers on the train of romantic and sexual pleasure. We felt full of confidence and vitality when we boarded at the beginning of the trip. We took our seat in the engine compartment and felt proud as we called the orders to get the train moving. But as the trip progressed we seemed to need more and more fuel to keep the train going. Our romantic desire was the fuel that kept the train rolling. Strangely, though, the more we fed our desire, the more hungry it became.

Slowly at first, then faster and faster, the train moved along. Gradually, we lost our position in the engineer's seat as the train gathered speed. We were thrown farther back, but still needed to provide the fuel to keep the train going. Finally, we found ourselves holding on to the caboose for dear life, knowing that if we kept trying to fuel the train with our lust we would die, but afraid that if we stopped and let go, we would surely fall to our death.

This is the final dilemma of the love addict. We can't stop engaging in romantic and sexual behaviors we know are killing us, but we are convinced that if we do stop we will die.

Fortunately, Carol was already in recovery for her alcoholism, and though it took her two years to recognize that sexual compulsion was now endangering her life as alcohol had once done, she reached out for help again.

The experiences of Roger and Carol are not unusual. Though love addiction has been ignored until recently, it is now gaining wider attention. Many believe we are at the same stage in our understanding of love addiction as we were forty years ago in our knowledge of alcoholism.

Characteristics of a Love Addict

No one becomes a love addict by accident. As we see in the lives of Carol, Roger, and many others, love addiction grows out of our beliefs about ourselves and the feelings we have about those closest to us. Becoming aware of these beliefs and feelings is crucial for our recovery. They are formed early in life, based on our need to survive in our families, and are continually reinforced as our addictions progress.

The following characteristics are typical of men and women who are love addicts, people like Carol and Roger and perhaps like you, too.

1. *Typically, you come from a home in which your needs for safety and security were not met.*
2. *Feeling unsafe and insecure, you grow up feeling like an orphan.*
3. *Never having felt safe to be who you really are, you develop an attractive image or facade with which you hope you will attract the kind of person you feel you need.*
4. *Looking good on the outside, you build up more and more pain on the inside. You go from one romantic intrigue to the next, hoping to block out the pain.*
5. *Afraid of being abandoned or abused, you seek a partner who is safe.*
6. *You search desperately for someone who will love and accept you, a person you can feel safe with, but deep down inside you don't believe anyone can be trusted.*
7. *Although you present an attractive and loving facade, inside you are filled with rage—rage at your love object for never giving you the care you so desperately need, and rage at yourself for needing that care.*
8. *The rage turned outward causes you to become manipulative, calculating, and mean. The rage turned within causes you to feel depressed and even suicidal.*

9. *You confuse basic needs for safety, security, love, and self-esteem with the need for romantic intrigue or sexual conquest.*

10. *Feeling you must have romantic contact in order to survive, but afraid that it would not be freely given, you develop a feeling of "sexual entitlement."*

11. *You feel unloved and unlovable. Trying to "be someone" and to "be cared for" when you can't be yourself, you feel more and more worthless.*

12. *You begin to rely more and more on a secret life as your addiction progresses.*

13. *You feel increasingly frightened and out of control as time goes on.*

14. *You know in your heart that you are looking for love in all the wrong places, but you don't know where to begin to look for what will truly satisfy you.*

15. *You have a desperate need to control people in your life, particularly the objects of your desire.*

16. *You may be predisposed emotionally and even biochemically to becoming addicted to drugs, alcohol, caffeine, nicotine, television, and/or certain foods, particularly sugary ones.*

17. *By being drawn constantly to situations of sexual and romantic intrigue, you avoid focusing on your inner fears and also avoid taking responsibility for your own life.*

18. *In spite of the pain and hopelessness you often feel, you don't give up. Somehow, you believe, there must be a better way to live.*

Roger and Carol exhibited nearly all of these characteristics. So, too, do most of the people I have seen over the years, both in the course of my own recovery and in my role as a psychotherapist specializing in treating addictive relationships.

Let's take a closer look now at the characteristics of love addiction:

1. *Typically, you come from a home in which your needs for safety and security were not met.*

The greatest sense of safety and security we can get is from parents who are able to understand and accept our feelings. When we feel understood on a deep level, we feel safe. But often our feelings are not accepted. We are told to be "big boys" and not cry when we are hurt. We are told to be "nice" to Aunt Sophie when we really feel like hitting her. We are told we don't need to suck our thumb anymore, and besides it will ruin our teeth. We are told that little "ladies" sit quietly.

Love addicts grow up feeling afraid. The world doesn't feel safe and we don't feel at home in the world.

Sometimes we come from families in which we were directly threatened, at other times we feel the indirect fear of a missing parent. Homes where safety and security needs were not met are those in which one or more of the following occur:

- one or both parents are absent either through death, divorce, or unusually long working hours
- parents abuse alcohol and/or drugs (prescribed or illicit)
- parents compulsively eat, work, clean, gamble, spend, diet, exercise, etc.
- parents show extreme rigidity about money, religion, work, sex, rules, etc.
- violence (either physical or emotional) is directed at a spouse and/or children
- physical or emotional illness is present in a parent
- a parent, stepparent, or guardian displays inappropriate sexual behavior toward a child, ranging from mild seductiveness to incest
- parents display extreme passivity about rules and expectations, providing little structure to allow the child to feel safe
- unclear and chaotic interaction exists between parents who are separated or divorced; children often feel caught in the middle and never know where their "home" is.

The dominant emotion these conditions foster is fear, and the child's basic motivation becomes to find the safety and security he or she needs in order to survive. Sex, drugs, alcohol, overwork, and other mind-modifiers dull the pain, provide momentary pleasure, and provide a spurious sense of safety.

Whatever the particular family experience, children who grow up in "unpredictable" environments become fearful of people and of the world "out there" and desperately seek the security they lacked growing up.

2. *Feeling unsafe and insecure, you grow up feeling like an orphan.*

Because our parents were "not there" for us in the most basic ways, we feel parentless and alone. It seems to us that we live in a dog-eat-dog world, where people are either victims or victimizers. We justify our misdeeds against others as realistic because you must "do unto others before they do unto you."

We feel powerless in the world and we yearn to return to a primal state of innocence in which our every need will be met by an all-loving mother and father. Psychoanalyst Bruno Bettelheim summarized what the orphan hopes for as a degree of acceptance in which "nothing is asked of us and all that we want is given."[2]

Another reason for this yearning to be cared for is our sense of abandonment and loss. No mother is perfect and every child must experience disappointments. We feel we are supposed to live in a garden, safe and cared for, but too often instead we feel thrown out into the wilderness, prey to unknown dangers.[3]

No matter how much we may strive to be successful in the world or to be a loving mate or parent, we are severely limited by the pain we feel as orphans. The pain mandates that we are almost totally self-absorbed. Our entire life centers around ourselves. We feel it must if we are to survive.

Since we never felt safe as children, we could never trust that we would find love and gentleness or make a real difference in the world. We settled, instead, for controlling the terms of our own unhappiness. We chose love addiction.

3. *Never having felt safe to be who you really are, you develop an attractive image or facade with which you hope you will attract the kind of person you feel you need.*

In our families we learned that it wasn't safe to be who we really were. Crying about a broken ashtray might result in a boy being ridiculed as a "sissy." Getting angry at mommy might cause her to hit or threaten her little girl.

Growing up we felt different. We never felt quite like other kids, yet we had a desperate need to belong and fit in. We became masters at "looking good," while inside we felt "bad." We learned how to hide our true feelings beneath a carefully constructed mask of acceptability. We each developed our own "thing" that made us appear valuable.

Some of us developed our good looks. We wore the right clothes and dressed in the proper style. We drove the "in" car and went with the "in" crowd. Some of us developed a style of being "different." Our heroes were the James Dean types, rebels without a cause. But we weren't really rebels. We spent hours looking in the mirror getting just the "right" look of indifference. And we weren't living lives that were wild and free. Rather we were looking for a special someone who would respond to our look.

Some of us became artists or businessmen. Many of us became doctors, therapists, social workers, and spiritual healers. We became salesmen and senators, policemen and politicians. Whatever our "thing," we did it with a vengeance.

We wore our masks well and developed an appealing look. We were "good with people." We were attractive, well-liked, and respected. We were asked to join school boards and sit on committees. We spoke out against social injustice. We became community leaders. Our opinions were sought on matters of importance. We were outraged about sexual abuse, frantic in our concern about the rising cost of teen pregnancy, fearful about the spread of AIDS. Few noticed that in our social preoccupations, love and sex played such a prominent role.

4. *Looking good on the outside, you build up more and more pain on the inside. You go from one sexual or romantic encounter to the next, hoping to block out the pain.*

We are always on the make, searching for our next conquest. We can't really enjoy the person we're with because we're already thinking about the next one to come along. We may tell ourselves that it's great to have so many friends, so many lovers. But we are never comfortable with what we have. The addict always wants just one more.

Underneath the calm exterior is a frightened animal. We've got to have more because we're never sure this one won't leave us. We live with a general terror that we must keep moving, looking.

Listen to the words of people who have been exploring their love addictions for some time. Feel the panic, as they remember their constant search for romantic intrigue.

"I had an affair or romantic flirtation going at almost all times. It had become a major part of who I was, it was the spice that made life interesting. It was my fix."

"It had never been my style to pick up people in bars or on the street, so I had to make sure that I was in contact with a lot of people to assure the opportunity would come up frequently. I worked two jobs and had a social life that was frantic and crazy."

"I was constantly searching for a person who was a combination whore/madonna, a woman who could give me sexual oblivion yet speak to my soul."

"I truly couldn't imagine a life without the excitement of 'falling in love.' Even more important than the physical contact was the thrill of the chase, the excitement of seeing who I would be with the next night or the next weekend. I was hooked on the thrill of making it all fit together without getting caught."

Eventually, we get tired of cruising and want more than anything else to find someone we can settle down with.

5. *Afraid of being abandoned or abused, you seek a partner who is safe.*

Once we have someone interested in us, someone we think we can trust, we do everything we can to get them hooked. We send flowers and candy. We leave little love notes on the windshield of their car. We are always available to help them, to give them a shoulder to cry on.

Persons not enmeshed in love addiction will find us too good to be true. But we make sure we pick someone who is also a love addict, someone desperately hungry—someone who will need us more than we need them. That, we believe, is our only security.

Once they are "ours," we do everything we can to make sure they remain ours. We shower our partner with "all that they could ever need or want." We want to be sure that they come to depend on us. We don't want them to get too close, though, since no one is really reliable.

Since we can't believe anyone would truly want to stay with us out of choice, we feel the only way we can hold on to them is to do a good job of selling ourselves. Only when we are totally convinced that they are "hooked" on us can we relax.

"I figured that I had her hooked, and that I could remain uncommitted without fear of losing her," said one man. "She seemed incapable of leaving me." While there's always the need to keep the person hooked, we're always worried at the same time about letting ourselves get too close and hence becoming vulnerable. Our lives are a constant series of ups-and-downs.

6. *You search desperately for someone who will love and accept you, a person you can feel safe with, but deep down inside you don't believe anyone can be trusted.*

We often forget that our parents were our first "lovers." They were the ones closest to us. We lived in intimate contact with them and depended on them for our physical and emotional survival. Whatever was unresolved with our parents, we try to re-create and resolve with our adult lovers.

As children our world was unpredictable and hence unsafe. Whether our parents were alcoholic, mentally ill, or rigidly moralistic, they weren't able to give us the stable, consistent care we needed.

We never knew, at so young an age, that they had problems that made it impossible for them to be consistently supportive of us. We never knew that parents represent only two people in the world. For us they represented the *whole* world. If I can't trust them, then I can't trust anyone. If my parents can't "see" me, I must be invisible and worthless.

We believe that, as one addict put it, "to know me is to leave me." Like two porcupines in the snow, we want desperately to get close for the comfort and warmth necessary to survive, but when we start to snuggle, we are afraid of being pierced by the other's quills and pull quickly away.

The closer we get to someone the more frightened we become as our vulnerability stimulates the old fear. We run away, but quickly feel depressed and lonely and need to get back fast. We feel like a yo-yo or that we are doomed to ride a violent, out-of-control roller coaster for the rest of our lives.

7. *Although you present an attractive and loving facade, inside you are filled with rage—rage at your love object for never giving you the care you so desperately need, and rage at yourself for needing that care.*

When we were children our needs were constant, and they couldn't be turned on and off to suit our parents' availability to meet them.

We were abused children. Yet many of us didn't consider ourselves abused because our parents didn't beat us, or sexually abuse us, or starve us. For us the abuse was more subtle: A child, lonely for his father, because his mother was afraid to let anyone else touch "her" baby; a girl, treated like a little doll by her parents, who learned very early the proper role for a young lady; a little girl who was held too closely by a father who wanted her to give him the love he was not getting from his wife; a boy made to stay in a dark closet to make him overcome his fear of the dark.

Whatever the degree of abuse, we build up anger, which turns to rage as it is buried more and more deeply inside. This happens because as children we believed that to express our anger would result in our being abandoned or abused even more.

The rage still lurks inside us as adults. We learn to hate the lover who never can give us enough, and we learn to hate ourselves for being so dependent on what they do give.

8. *The rage turned outward causes you to become manipulative, calculating, and mean. The rage turned within causes you to feel depressed and even suicidal.*

Underneath our calm exterior we are often down and depressed, the result of our anger turning inward. We may even feel suicidal.

39

We often use romance as an antidepressant, seeking the excitement of romantic intrigue to overcome our inner feelings of deadness.

One recovering love addict remembers the horrors of the past: "I used love to survive the depression that immobilized me. I constantly used romance to give me a sense of aliveness and excitement. It was a roller coaster of fear and lust, but the thrill of secret adventure and new lovers seemed to keep me from feeling down all the time and I didn't want to stop."

Rage turned outward causes us to use people for our own ends. Sometimes we go to prostitutes. Other times we buy favors from our lovers by showering them with gifts and affection. Often we aren't even aware that we are manipulating others. A thirty-eight-year-old man, two years in recovery, was finally able to see the truth of his behavior: "I would kid myself into believing that all the women I saw were 'friends.' I convinced myself that they were really important in my life, that I really cared for them as people. Yet if they didn't have sex with me, I would seldom see them for fun, just when I was lonely or needy."

A forty-four-year-old woman looked back on how she used men throughout her life: "As a teenager I used my sexuality by teasing men enough to obtain favors, but not going all the way. Later I lived with Henry. I was revolted every time he touched me. But Henry loved what I had—a female body—and I loved what he had—money, power, assertiveness, and a weakness through which he could be manipulated."

Since we are afraid to express our real needs, we become more and more devious. We create elaborate stories to cover our mistakes. We will do anything, say anything, lie, cheat, or steal in order to get what we need. Sometimes we lose control of ourselves and our anger explodes.

After a violent outburst we feel terribly confused and guilty. We don't understand where our anger comes from. Our love object seems so guiltless, it makes us even more depressed and miserable. We see our partner as an innocent victim and ourselves as bad and mean.

We are blind to the fact that our explosive anger toward our partner is a re-creation of what was done to us as children to keep us quiet. In working with men who batter women, I found that every abusive man had himself been abused as a child. They had either been hit, threatened with violence, or been put in isolation. As adults, they may hit their partner when their frustration over-flows; they may threaten—"Shut up, bitch, or I'll knock your god-damn head off!" or they may isolate—"I can't deal with you. I'm getting out of here!" Few are even aware that they are re-creating what was done to them as children.

Violence should not be condoned no matter what the cause. But it helps us understand our rage and be able to control it when we recognize that we're not inherently mean. We learned to be that way. Therefore we can learn to change.

9. *You confuse basic needs for safety, security, love, and self-esteem with the need for romantic intrigue or sexual conquest.*

Normally a person's needs for survival, safety, and security would be fairly well met before he or she reached adulthood. There would be a firm base from which to develop love and self-esteem. Love addicts, however, never developed a basic sense of security. They are children in adult bodies, going through the motions of finding love. But they don't have the proper tools for the job.

In our attempt to survive, we believe that if we could just connect with the right romantic partner or consummate the next sexual encounter, all our needs would be met including those for safety, security, love, and self-esteem.

Therefore we become terrified when a partner doesn't give us the romantic response we expect. We're not just adults upset be-cause we didn't get our treat. We're adult-children who believe we will *cease to exist* without the romantic contact.

10. *Feeling you must have romantic contact in order to survive, but afraid that it will not be freely given, you develop a feeling of "sexual entitlement."*

41

All of us who are addicted to love, particularly men, have within us an irrational desire for "contact on demand." If we could go inside a man's head and listen to his most honest feelings about women we might hear something like this: "I want a woman of my own, whom I can command, and who will respond willingly, to comfort me in my lack and loneliness."

Surely we can all sympathize with such a plea. All of us would like to be taken care of by an always-available, all-comforting mother. But those of us who are addicted to love go beyond merely wanting it to a feeling that we *must* have it.

We make demands on our partners as though we were entitled to their favors. Women are not simply women, they symbolize the need men have to capture the life force. Men aren't simply men, they represent the power women feel they must have in order to survive.

11. *You feel unloved and unlovable. Trying to "be someone" and to "be cared for" when you can't be yourself, you feel more and more worthless.*

To feel lovable we must first have a good sense of ourselves, yet many of us never had the kind of nurturing attention as children that lets us know we are valued.

We all had the cord cut when we were born. But many of us didn't develop a separate sense of ourselves. We were told in many ways that our "self" didn't exist.

One of my clients, Rebecca, whose parents called her "Dolly," reflected on her feelings growing up. "I never felt quite 'solid.' There was always a feeling of semi-invisibility, like I wasn't made of real substance. I never felt I had my own boundaries. It was like I had a zipper down the front of my body. Someone could always pull it down and reach inside me."

No matter how fast we run, how hard we try, how much we achieve, how many conquests we make, inside we feel worthless. We develop ever more elaborate trappings to entice people to us, but our secret fear is that below the surface is a black hole. We feel like an empty shell.

12. *You begin to rely more and more on a secret life as your addiction progresses.*

From the time we were children, we couldn't rely on our parents for consistent support and comfort, so we learned early to rely on our fantasies. They were always there for us. They became more real to us than the "real" world. "Out there" seemed dangerous and unpredictable, so we learned to go inside where the world was always sweet. Inside our minds, we were in charge, we controlled who came and went.

When we discovered the joys of sexual pleasure our inner world took on a new level of intensity and excitement. Childhood dreams gradually turned into adult fantasies. Most of us are familiar with male magazines such as *Playboy* and *Penthouse*. Many are not aware that there is a vast collection of female literature—the romance novel—that serves the same purpose for women.[4]

When our fantasies begin getting played out in reality, we need to keep this side of our lives secret as well. We are ashamed of our behavior and as protective of our "private lives" as we are of our fantasies. They can remain safe if we keep others away.

13. *You feel increasingly frightened and out of control as time goes on.*

Love addiction is progressive. It gets worse over time. What begins as pleasure, a simple way to make us feel good, becomes a compulsion that seems to take on a life of its own. Lust always requires novel experience. As we continue to seek the new and exciting, our world becomes more chaotic and fearful.

Listen to the reports of a number of men and women in recovery who reflect back on the loss of control they felt as their sexual addiction progressed.

"When I was in the arms of a man, I felt a beautiful oblivion, and it was all I wanted. But now I was starting to get the sense that I was oblivion's victim."

*   *   *

"The addiction destroyed my marriage. It always came first, even before my own security. Living with others, much less being responsible, was impossible."

"We had very little in common; I knew even then that I didn't particularly like him, but I remember saying to a friend, I can't get out of this relationship. He's too good in bed."

"My life had gotten completely out of control with an endless series of compulsive romantic activities. My addictive appetite never seemed to get enough."

Bill, a thirty-five-year-old sexual addict in recovery, sums up the feelings many of us wrestle with as we come to grips with our addiction: "The possibility that no durable happiness or fulfillment could ever come from living out this pointless pattern did not occur to me at all. The promise of the 'next one' being the perfect person who at last was going to make me whole was the promise that seemed to be forever dancing in front of me, coaxing me ever onward."

14. *You know in your heart that you are looking for love in all the wrong places, but you don't know where to begin to look for what will truly satisfy you.*

We're like children who grow up on sweets. We know they aren't good for us, but we don't know how to find healthy food. We really have two related problems. The first is one of knowledge. Never having experienced real love in our families and having surrounded ourselves in adulthood with people who reflect the same distorted attitudes we grew up with, we don't really know what love is.

The second problem, and the more difficult one to treat, is that our deepest and most sacred beliefs about love are upside-down. For us love and pain got intertwined. We're like homing pigeons with a sickness that causes us to fly away from home rather than toward it. Then, the farther away we get, the more homesick we become, and the faster we fly away.

44

Love is based on being ourselves. Yet we have learned to wear masks and be someone we're not.

Love requires that we open ourselves to another. Yet we are too fearful to become vulnerable.

Love requires that we see the beauty in another. Yet we see others only as objects of our lust.

Love, as Dr. Gerald Jampolsky says, is letting go of fear.[5] Yet we believe that only our fears keep us alive.

15. *You have a desperate need to control people in your life, particularly the objects of your desire.*

Control is important in all areas of the love addict's life. The only time we can feel safe is when we are in charge. Loss of control is terrifying. Our jobs, our homes, our friends and children—all must be under our wing for us to feel safe. Nowhere is this need to control more evident than in our intimate relationships.

Secretly we feel that if the object of our desire were not under our control, he or she would surely leave us or otherwise harm us. We need to "possess" our love objects because they seem essential to our survival.

We've always got to have a lover even if we're so busy at work we don't have time for them or live so far away that we never see them. It's vital that we simply know they are *there*.

16. *You may be predisposed emotionally and even biochemically to becoming addicted to drugs, alcohol, caffeine, nicotine, television, and/or certain foods, particularly sugary ones.*

Each time I attend a 12-step meeting it's obvious that we are "generic addicts." There isn't anything unique about our relationship to alcohol, gambling, or sex. We are addictive personality types and therefore are vulnerable to becoming hooked on anything that blocks out pain and produces an altered state of consciousness.

We need to recognize that many addicts have more than one primary addiction. Many rehabilitative programs focus only on one addiction in the mistaken belief that once the specific addiction is

45

taken care of other problem behaviors will disappear. Many love addicts have been told this, and their lives have been needlessly endangered because they didn't deal with their love addiction.

A forty-year-old man, six years sober in AA, said: "In AA I kept hearing, 'Don't drink, go to meetings, and your life will get better.' In the next nine years, I didn't drink, went to well over two thousand AA and Al-Anon meetings, worked the 12 Steps to the best of my ability, and my life kept on unraveling." He finally realized that dealing with his alcoholism wasn't enough. He needed to deal with his love addiction as well.

If you find that you have had problems with one addiction, keep a close watch on the way you relate to other situations even if looking at them is painful.

A number of researchers in the field of addictions have suggested that all addictions are in fact related and that people who are susceptible to any one will be susceptible to others.[6] I believe our understanding of addictions has been misguided until recently. We have spent too much time concentrating on the qualities of the specific addictive substance and not enough time on the qualities that predispose us to all kinds of addictions.

Thomas Szasz says that trying to understand drug addiction by concentrating primarily on drugs makes about as much sense as trying to understand holy water by studying the water.[7] To understand holy water we must know about priests and parishioners, not water; to understand addictions, we must examine addicts and helpers, families and friends.

17. *By being drawn constantly to situations of sexual and romantic intrigue, you avoid focusing on your inner fears and also avoid taking responsibility for your own life.*

The more we engage in sexual and romantic intrigue the farther away we get from our true selves. In fact, we are terrified to look inside. Our fear is that we would find a horrible beast that would devour us. Even greater is our fear that inside our shell there is nothing. The terror of nothingness is what keeps us addicted to the pain that our love lives now cause us.

Once we have been able to be honest about our out-of-control behavior, we wonder why we don't stop. Sometimes we think we must be going absolutely crazy. Why would people do this to themselves unless they were insane?

What we often fail to realize is that years of role playing have left us totally out of touch with ourselves. Inside we feel dead. At least pain lets us know we are alive.

We began our love addiction as a way of protecting ourselves from pain. Now we have become addicted to pain itself. We hold on to it to survive. We developed our addiction as a means of protecting ourselves, but found we lost ourselves in the process. We started our addiction as a way to take control of our own lives, yet now we have become ever more irresponsible in dealing with ourselves and other people.

18. *In spite of the pain and hopelessness you often feel, you don't give up. Somehow, you believe, there must be a better way to live.*

Love addicts are survivors. We survived abusive childhoods and destructive adult relationships. The kinds of experiences that would have killed some drove us on. We never gave up because somehow we knew there was a better way to live.

Even though our lives have been driven by fear, some part of us is always searching for love. We may have been looking for it in all the wrong places, but we have never given up looking for it.

So here's the good news: I believe that a whole-hearted commitment to anything will lead to love eventually. Addicts do not lead lives of "quiet desperation." We go after life with everything we have. Our obsession with love may have become destructive over time, but it has always been whole-hearted.

As a child I learned that there were two ways of seeing the truth. One was by seeing what it "was." The other was by seeing what it "was not."

I remember doing a kindergarten art project. We were asked to get a leaf from the yard. One part of the project had us drawing the outline of the leaf, then lifting it off the paper and painting in all the little veins and structures inside the leaf. The next part of the project was to place the leaf on paper, hold a piece of screen over the leaf, and run our paint brush over the screen. To our amazement, we found when we lifted off the screen that we got a perfect picture of the leaf made by all the little spots of paint that fell over the screen. Somehow that experiment from childhood became a metaphor for ways of seeing the world.

As love addicts, we became experts on knowing what love "was not." Each of us could write the definitive book on "how not to" find love. In beginning to confront our addiction, we also begin to realize that as "victims of love" we have actually learned a great deal about love. If we look at the artwork of our life as a perfect mess, seeing only all the "missed spots" that fell outside, we lose an incredible opportunity. Once we realize the mess is "our" mess and in fact it is "perfect," we lift off the leaf and see the beautiful outline of love we have created. We can then begin the next step of filling it in.

To make that "flip" of the leaf requires only one thing. We must let go of our belief that we are alone in the world, doomed to die because no one has ever loved us.

Hugh Prather, in his introduction to *Love Is Letting Go of Fear,* tells this touching story: "A man who had finished his life went before God. And God reviewed his life and showed him the many lessons he had learned. When He had finished, God said, 'My child, is there anything you wish to ask?' And the man said, 'While You were showing me my life, I noticed that when the times were pleasant there were two sets of footprints, and I knew You walked beside me. But when times were difficult there was only one set of footprints. Why, Father, did You desert me during the difficult times?' And God said, 'You misinterpret, my son. It is true that when the times were pleasant I walked beside you and pointed out the way. But when the times were difficult, I carried you.'"[8]

Whether or not we believe in God, we do believe most deeply in love. All it takes to begin our journey toward love and away from uncontrolled and obsessive romance and sex is a willingness to stop blaming ourselves and others for our situation. We can then drop our masks and reach out to another human being, as our true selves.

48

No matter how lonely you may feel, you do not walk alone. As you move beyond your fears and begin once again to trust in people, you will see support all around you. Perhaps you will realize this as you continue to read further in this book. Please know that what it contains is offered with love, from someone who has "been there" and cares about you.

2. THE ENDLESS SEARCH FOR LOVE

Janis Joplin: Victim of Love

"Too much ain't enough!" These are the words of one of the legends of modern rock/blues music, one of the most extraordinary singers and personalities of the 60's. The example of Janis Joplin's life can help us understand the behavior of love addicts.

In his biography of the star, author David Dalton wrote: "Janis insisted on following the bright, colorblind, toenail party of love. Like the fantasy worlds of Gothic Romances and Coke commercials, her notion of love was of such excessive proportions, so extreme and absurd, that it transcended not just the real world but also any real possibility of satisfaction."[1]

Janis died alone in her room at the Landmark Hotel in Los Angeles on October 4, 1970, at 1:40 A.M. The autopsy concluded that the cause of death had been an overdose of heroin and alcohol.

I've come to see that Janis, and so many others like her, died from drug use, but that her real addiction was to love. In getting a glimpse into the life of Janis Joplin, perhaps we can come to understand our own.

I smiled sadly when I remembered seeing Janis at The Avalon, in San Francisco, interspersing her songs with swigs from a bottle of Southern Comfort. But she couldn't find the real solace that she had missed as a child growing up in Port Arthur, Texas.

Dalton says of her that she "wanted to make up for the pain of a lifetime in one love affair . . . and it always seemed like singing would deliver this phantom, fictional lover to her tonight and nothing would ever part them again."[2]

As love addicts, we too want to make up for the pain of a lifetime in one magnificent love affair. We too seem always to be moving toward that magical "something" and away from where we really are. We never seem to find it, yet we aren't able to stop long enough to question our direction. The farther away from real love we get, the more we get lost in our fantasy of love. We become "moonlight gamblers" forever placing our bets on the next "big spin" of love.

Janis got hooked on the phantom lovers she created in her music. "Real lovers," Dalton says, "were something that threatened to drag one back into the sordid details and banal resolutions of everyday life, and specimens of manhood as preposterous as those Janis invokes in her lyrics could only exist in songs. Her real-life lovers, even the most intense of them, were disposable, as if the actuality of romance was somehow a debasement, a crude mundane metaphor for her conception of what romance must be."[3]

Wounded as children, we are afraid to take the risk of getting close enough to develop real love. Our passions and desires can be safely expressed only in fantasy, and "sex" becomes the perfect fantasy. One man in recovery, reflecting on his childhood, had this to say: "Looking back today with the help of therapy, I can see that I was a physically and emotionally abused child. When I discovered sexuality I fell in love with it." About his adult life he acknowledged the two themes of fear and desire: "I looked for situations where I could experience sexual contact without emotional entanglements—sex without commitment."

Janis once said about her sexual desire, "I'm saving the bass player for Omaha."[4] On the surface she was indifferent to sex, yet in her behavior there was a driven quality, a need to have someone close by all the time, even if just a warm body in bed.

We can feel the restless, bittersweet search of the romantic and sexual addict when Janis sings "Bobby McGee." "One can imagine Janis as one of those possessed, imprinted birds pumping her wings furiously, ceaselessly across Texas, New Mexico, Arizona, California," Dalton says, "ignoring the seductions of the cowboys, oil riggers and semi drivers waving their hats to her from below, driven onwards, and, always, inexorably, away. The states reflected in her eyes as she pants, 'Got to get there, got to get there, got to get there, gotta, gotta get there.' "[5]

We can feel the child's longing to be held. We can feel the child's faith that somewhere, somehow, she can find the love she needs. But as she expresses her childhood optimism that "if I could just do it right" everything would be okay, she is also expressing the childhood fear and desire for flight.

As we run faster and faster to get away from our childhood fears, we get farther and farther away from our only true source of love— ourselves.

Those addicts who have acquired fame and fortune are visible to the public, but still they seem distant from us. In chapter 1 we met some ordinary people whose lives had become disrupted as a result of their romantic addictions. Let's meet a few more now so that we can get a feeling of the range of experiences that constitute romantic addiction.

"My Fantasies Interfere with My Work"

Richard—thirty-two; licensed psychologist; married, with two children: "I became a psychologist because I wanted to help people and I'm sure, on some level, to work out some of my own hangups from childhood. I've always had a strong desire to have a family. I met my wife when we were both students in college. We married young and had two children in succession.

"When the kids were small she stayed home and I rapidly rose in my field of community mental health treatment. Things seemed to go well between us until the kids went off to school and Dorothy wanted to get a job. I was all for it, and still am, but she seemed to lose interest in me in her excitement to get herself established.

53

"As a psychotherapist, I'm familiar with patients always falling in love with their doctor. Although I've been tempted a few times in the past, I could always restrain myself. I'd remind myself about my professional ethics, the needs of the patient, and my own happy home. Lately I can't keep my eyes, and sometimes my hands, off women who come to see me. I'm elated when a new client is an attractive woman and disappointed when it's a man. I look for ways to hold on to her hand a little longer when we touch to say good-bye. God, I even find myself losing track of what a particularly attractive patient is saying. I find I'm thinking about what she would be like with her dress pulled up and me making love to her on the couch.

"I haven't acted on these fantasies, but I can't seem to stop them. I know many other people in the helping professions—psychiatrists, psychologists, social workers, clergy—who are having the same problem. Some I know have slept with their clients. Some justify it as 'therapeutic,' while others candidly admit that it is wrong, but that they can't control themselves.

"Sometimes I think it wouldn't be so bad to go all the way. Maybe I would get it out of my system. Yet I know what I'm doing is dangerous and I feel terribly guilty about taking money from clients while I'm lusting after them in my mind. I got into this field to help people and now I think it's me who needs help."

"I Seem to Attract Men Who Like to Scare Me"

Jennifer—thirty; buyer for a large department store; single: "Most men think I am pretty and I never have had a problem getting dates. Yet I still feel like the chubby girl with glasses I remember from my fourth-grade picture. I could go out every night if I wanted to accept all the invitations I get, but the problem is the kind of men that are attracted to me.

"They always look good, at first. They are handsome, well dressed, intelligent, and successful. But invariably we get involved in some kind of dangerous romantic activity. I had been going out with this one guy, Tom, for about a month and he seemed like a really nice man. One night after going to a movie we took a walk in the park.

54

The moon was out and it was very romantic. We stopped and sat under a tree. As we kissed and became more excited, it became clear that Tom wanted to make love right out in the open. I wanted to go back to my apartment.

"I remember feeling really scared. This was a park where people had been assaulted and I felt uncomfortable and very vulnerable. But somehow I couldn't say no even though I was scared to death. Tom seemed to like the excitement and said he enjoyed the possibility of getting caught.

"I don't know why, but I seem to attract men who like to scare me. The more frightened I get, the more excited they become. One man I was really crazy about and almost married liked to run a knife down my body when we made love. At times I thought he might hurt me if I didn't go along with him. At other times he would laugh, say he was just joking, and become the most gentle man around.

"I never was sure whether I was attracted to his gentleness or the violence that seemed to be just below the surface. I don't know why I keep attracting men like this, but it's beginning to worry me."

"I'm Worried but I Still Continue"

Linda—forty-four; housewife; married, with three grown children: "We just celebrated our twenty-fifth wedding anniversary. Bob bought me diamonds and told me I was still as attractive as when I was a beauty queen in college. We met and married during our freshman year. The babies came quickly and I eventually dropped out of college to be a momma. Luckily Bob's family had money and they were very generous with us.

"Our love life was always good, but it never totally satisfied me. From the time I was a little girl I always had a rich fantasy life. It always seemed to help me feel safe when Mom and Dad fought, mostly after he had been drinking. I think I learned to pleasure myself when I was seven or eight years old and from then on I always loved fantasy. As I got older I found that men were attracted to me and I guess you could say I was a little tease. I'd run around the house in my underwear and drive my older brother to distraction.

"In high school I was a romance novel junkie. I'd read them for hours and create elaborate fantasies about being ravished by strange men, usually in uniform. I never had a lot of friends in school and I never told anyone about my fantasies. Going to college helped me gain some independence from my family. But I still lived at home and it wasn't until Bob came along that I could really get out completely.

"When the children were young, Bob was embarrassed about my 'running around bare-assed.' He said it wasn't good for the kids to see me naked. I felt it was a little strange myself, so I began to indulge my fantasies when I was alone. When Bob was away at work I found myself spending time alone fantasizing about men— the gardener, the mailman, the grocer, just about anyone. I started developing a kind of ritual. I'd get the kids up and out, take a bubble bath, then sit down with a novel. Sometime during the day I would seek out some man and just kind of act provocatively. I'd never wanted to really get something going with them. If they came on to me, I'd act surprised and pretend to be offended. Then I'd come home and touch myself.

"I'd also change clothes a number of times during the day. Usually I'd do it in front of a window and 'accidentally' leave the curtain open. It would excite me to think of men passing by who could see me. I find now, though, that I need newer and more intense stimulation to give me the same high I used to get. I'm beginning to worry that someone might break in and rape me, but I still continue.

"One thing happened recently that really made me stop and think. One evening, just before Bob got home, I heard a knock at the door. Two police officers identified themselves. I was terrified. I had been 'changing clothes' in the bedroom and I was sure they were coming to arrest me. They said they had caught a man in the shrubbery beside the house looking in the window. I hadn't even known he was there. They wanted to know if I wanted to press charges. I was so scared I told them I would. Afterwards I just cried and shook. When Bob came home he comforted and consoled me about my trauma. All I could think about was the man I had sent to jail."

"I'm Hooked on Him and Don't Know What To Do"

Barbara—forty years old; married, with one grown child: "My husband, John, and I have been married for twenty-two years and in many ways it has been an ideal marriage. We love each other very much and are proud that we married young and have stayed together all these years. Our son is just graduating college and he has gotten a job with the state of Minnesota in their data processing department. My husband works in the same department and hopes that our son will take over for him when he retires in four more years.

"Everything in our lives had been going smoothly until I met Jason three years ago.

"After being the traditional housewife for the first ten years of our marriage, I got a job as a secretary for a group of architects. I loved getting out of the house, and the field of architectural design was fascinating. As the business grew I took on more and more responsibility for setting up meetings with new clients, making flight arrangements, hotel reservations, and generally organizing the business.

"Three years ago I took the plunge and went into business for myself. At first John was afraid that we wouldn't be able to make it financially, but I became very successful very quickly. I planned meetings for a number of large businesses. I thought John would be proud of me, but the more successful I became, the more he seemed to withdraw. Our love life suffered and we made love less and less and only when he was interested.

"In spite of the difficulties, I never thought of leaving John or going out with anyone else. I love him and our life is generally quite happy.

"Jason is the personnel director for one of the companies I consult

57

with. We met when we were assigned to develop plans for an important business conference in Europe. We were together constantly for a period of three months. It felt so good to have someone who really was interested in me and my work. We would spend hours talking about our ideas for the company and our thoughts for the future. He felt like a brother, a colleague, and a friend, all wrapped up in one.

"We both talked about our romantic interest in each other, but agreed it wouldn't be a good idea to pursue it. We were both happily married. Well, our resolve didn't last long and the time we spent together was magical for me. We were in Europe for a week and spent the whole time working and making love.

"When we returned to the States I was totally in love. He felt like a second husband. I didn't want to leave John, but I couldn't bear the thought of losing Jason. I was happy to let things go on the way they were. But Jason said we would have to stop seeing each other, that our involvement was beginning to interfere with our work. I agreed in words, but in my heart I felt I would die. I tried to accept the ending, it made logical sense to me, but the more I tried to get him out of my mind the more preoccupied I became.

"I would go out of my way to run into him at the office, even began following him after work. I hated myself for my weakness, but I couldn't stop myself. I couldn't believe that he didn't want me as much as I wanted him. I felt like I was going crazy. I would get angry at him, write him nasty letters that I would immediately tear up, and swear that I never wanted to see him again. The next day I would be ecstatically happy if I caught a glimpse of him walking down the hall.

"I feel hooked and I don't know what do do. All my good sense tells me to forget him and get on with my life, but I seem incapable of letting go."

"Fatal Attraction"

Joe—thirty-eight; stockbroker; divorced: "I just saw the movie *Fatal Attraction* for the third time. I feel like I continue to attract these

58

kinds of women in my life and I'm trying to figure out why that is.

"It's never gone so far that the woman tries to kill me, but I know the feeling of being with a woman who can explode at any minute. Jill is a doctor and spends her time helping cure other people of their various illnesses. I was attracted to her, initially, because of her fantastic energy and joy in life. She was always on the go, excited about doing things, and extremely loving and romantic.

"Our first two months together were some of the happiest in my life. But lately it's like living in the middle of a bad dream. Jill is very demanding of my attention and if she feels slighted, she goes wild. One night recently we went to a party some friends were having. We came in separate cars because Jill had to work late at the clinic. We'd had a few drinks and were socializing. I thought things were fine, but I looked over at Jill and she had that mean, angry look on her face, like I'd done something terrible.

"We went out on the balcony to talk and she lit into me, saying I didn't pay any attention to her and only cared about my friends. I was shocked. I didn't feel at all like I was neglecting her. The more I tried to explain, the angrier she got. Finally, she yelled something and ran out saying she was going home. At first I thought I better just let her go. But I was afraid something might happen to her driving in that state of mind so I went to catch up with her. I got there just as she was driving away. I went back to tell the host we were leaving, but when I got back to the car I found she had let all the air out of the tires.

"She drives me nuts. A month ago she got upset and threw my car keys in the bushes. It took me two hours to find them. Another time she burned some of my favorite books. Sometimes I feel she's out to hurt me. At other times I feel sorry for her. She always apologizes and I think next time it will be different.

"After seeing the movie I wonder if I'm addicted to the highs and lows I get in the relationship. I realize my work is also a series of crises. When it's good, it's great and when it's bad it's terrible. I can't continue to live like this."

59

"I'm Sure He'll Leave Me"

Jill—forty-one; physician; divorced: "I don't know why I treat Joe the way I do. I really love him. In fact he's the best thing that's happened in my life in a long time. Most of the time I feel fine and the relationship is wonderful. But there are times I start feeling insecure and then all hell breaks lose.

"It doesn't even have to be anything Joe does, though I know I blame him for his lack of attention. It's like a black cloud passes over me and I feel totally alone and loveless. I feel I've got to have Joe's attention or I'm going to die. It seems irrational at times, even to me, but I don't seem to be able to do anything about it. I know when I'm feeling that way we're going to get into a fight. I can see it coming. I tell myself not to let it happen and I do it anyway.

"I know it's not all me. Joe can be extremely insensitive and hurtful, then look at me with those big blue, innocent eyes, as though he has no idea what he's done. It does drive me wild sometimes. I want to hurt him like he's hurt me. Afterwards, I feel very foolish and guilty and do everything I can to get him to forgive me. He usually does, but I'm afraid that someday I'm going to drive him away like I've done all the other men in my life. Sometimes I feel like I'm just a mean, hurtful bitch. I know I'll be left sooner or later, so I might as well get it over with.

"I want more than anything else in the world to stop being this way. I'm afraid if I told Joe how I really felt inside, he'd know I was crazy and leave me for sure. If I can convince him the fights are his fault, somehow I think he'll want to stay.

"I know a lot of this has to do with my father leaving me when I was a little girl. I've never really been able to forgive him for running off. Knowing I've got a lot of left-over anger towards men doesn't seem to help me change things."

"I'm Starving Myself of Love"

Helen—forty-nine; librarian; divorced: "When Hank left me for a younger woman, I was devastated. We'd never had children and

I was completely devoted to him. He was tall and handsome, blond and blue-eyed. He was a real man. We married young and had a rich and satisfying love life. It felt like the ideal marriage. I was the envy of all my friends. When Hank left no one could believe it, but all my friends quickly wanted to fix me up with a new man.

"For a long time I didn't think I was ready, then I got very involved with a community group that was opposed to pornography. They were mostly professional people who felt pornography was degrading to women and added to the perception that it was okay to use and abuse women sexually. I've liked children, though I never had any of my own, and the more I got involved with the group, the more concerned I became about the effect of pornography on kids.

"When men would ask me out, I would decline, saying I was too busy with my work. But it's been fifteen years now since Hank left me and I haven't been out with a man. Everyone thinks it's strange and my friends are worried about me. I've begun to feel that there is something wrong. I know that being busy is just an excuse. I'm beginning to see that I never really got over Hank's leaving, or probably my father's death when I was nine years old.

"Many of my friends are obsessed with romance. All they can talk about is who they slept with or wanted to sleep with. I'm beginning to think that I'm also obsessed with romance, but in the opposite direction. I think about sex all the time. But I'm thinking about how repulsive sex is, how ugly and degrading it is. It's like all sensuality has become pornography in my mind.

"I've heard of people who become obsessed with food. Only instead of eating too much, they don't eat at all. They have 'anorexia' and starve themselves to death. I feel like I'm a sexual anorexic, like I'm starving myself of love. I may not die from lack of love, but my life has become terribly unhappy."

The key to understanding love addiction isn't to categorize what people do. This often leads to labeling behaviors we may not like or approve of as "sick" or "addictive." It's more useful to understand the patterns of behavior, the reasons people engage in them, and the effects the behavior has on themselves and others.

61

To do this requires that we look at addictive love from a number of different perspectives. Focusing directly on the addiction, we often miss its essence. We need instead to think of the addictive process on many levels, each level bringing us closer to the core of understanding. To do this we will explore what different self-help groups say about love addiction, how professionals view the problem, and we will also consider related addictions such as eating disorders and wealth addiction. As we explore, let yourself go, be willing to take a new look at your behavior and the behavior of those close to you.

Mutual-Support Groups

There are a number of mutual-support groups that base their programs on the principles of Alcoholics Anonymous. Each has a slightly different understanding of romantic and sexual addiction, but each can add to our understanding.

Sex and Love Addicts Anonymous describes the people who are members as suffering from a compulsive need for sex, and/or a desperate attachment to one person.[6] What all members have in common is an obsessive/compulsive pattern, either sexual, emotional, or both, in which relationships or activities have become increasingly destructive to all areas of their lives—career, family, and sense of self-respect.

The people in SLAA found that the compulsion to continue with promiscuous sex or to return over and over to a destructive relationship could not be controlled by willpower alone. By joining together, supporting each other, and following the 12 Steps, they found they were able to stop compulsive sexual behavior and develop healthy forms of loving relationships.

Prior to involvement in SLAA, many reported having tried other forms of help but nothing seemed to work. The lack of control people experienced was seen as proof that they were "bad" or defective people. They would seek comfort by justifying their behavior or by denying their sexuality altogether.

Sexaholics Anonymous (SA) says there is only one requirement for membership—a desire to stop lusting and become sexually sober.

Members call themselves sexaholics. The sexaholic, they say, has taken himself out of the whole context of what is right and wrong. He or she has lost control and no longer has the power of choice; these people are not free to stop. Like an alcoholic who can no longer tolerate alcohol in his system but is hooked and cannot stop drinking, the sexaholic can no longer tolerate lust but cannot stop sexual activity.

Sex Addicts Anonymous (SAA) describes itself as a group of men and women who share strength, hope, and experience with each other so they may overcome their sex addiction and help others to recover. Membership is open to all who share a desire to stop compulsive sexual behavior. Like the other two self-help programs just mentioned, the SAA program is based on the principles of Alcoholics Anonymous, but is not affiliated with AA.

Information on how to contact each of these programs can be found on page 204 of this book.

The Professional View

Patrick J. Carnes, in *Out of the Shadows*, also draws a parallel between love addiction and chemical addictions. He says that like an alcoholic, the love addict substitutes a sick relationship to an event or process for a healthy relationship with others. The addict's relationship with a mood-altering "experience" becomes central to his life.[7]

Dr. Eli Coleman, Associate Director of the Human Sexuality Program, University of Minnesota Medical School, points out the pattern of excesses, the lack of control, the amount of preoccupation, and the disruption of their lives that is characteristic of people who are having problems with their sexual relationships. Although not entirely comfortable with the term "sexual addiction" to describe these problems, he also utilizes some of the dynamics of other compulsive or addictive behaviors as criteria for sexual compulsivity.[8]

Coleman goes on to make an important distinction between healthy expressions of sexuality and unhealthy or destructive sexuality. He says that any sexual behavior can become compulsive. This understanding of sexual compulsivity avoids making value judgments about any type of sexual behavior. The pattern of the behavior, the motivation, and the result determine whether a behavior is healthy, abusive, or compulsive.

Dr. Stanton Peele was one of the first serious researchers to connect addiction with love. In his excellent book *Love and Addiction* he made clear the relationship between these two seemingly separate states of being.[9] He noted that love is an ideal vehicle for addiction because it can so exclusively claim a person's consciousness. If, to serve as an addiction, something must be both reassuring and consuming, then a love relationship is perfectly suited for the task. Addictive relationships are also patterned, predictable, and isolated. When a person goes to another with the aim of filling an inner void, the relationship quickly becomes the center of his or her life.

Peele says that an addiction exists when someone's attachment to a person or sensation lessens his appreciation or ability to deal with other things in his environment or in himself. The person becomes increasingly dependent on that attachment as his only source of gratification.

Peele sums up his view of love addiction by calling it a sterile, ingrown dependency relationship with another person who serves as the object of our need for security. He makes it clear that the addiction doesn't come from the "thing," whether the thing is a drug or another person. The core of addiction comes from the void we feel inside that continually calls out to be filled.

Romantic addictions would be difficult enough to treat if people engaged only in these activities. However, most addicts have problems with multiple addictive substances. It is important, therefore, to hear from experts who treat such problems as alcoholism, drug addiction, eating disorders, and wealth addiction.

Anne Wilson Schaef says, "An addiction is any process over which we are powerless. A sure sign of an addiction is the sudden need to deceive ourselves and others—to lie, deny, and cover up. An addiction is anything we feel tempted to lie about."[10] She goes on to say that an addiction is anything we are not willing to give up. But we must be willing to do so to be free of addiction. Like any serious disease, an addiction is progressive, and it will lead to death unless we actively recover from it.

Schaef was one of the first people to understand that addictions were much more prevalent in our society than commonly believed. As long as addiction theory was focused only on chemicals we missed a lot of other addictive behavior because we never looked for it.

She describes two categories of addictions, both of which produce essentially the same results in an individual. The "substance addictions" or "ingestive addictions" concern alcohol, drugs, and food. In "process addictions" people get hooked on gambling, work, religion, worry, accumulating money, and sexual promiscuity. She points out that it isn't the substance or process that is so important; rather it is the addict's relationship to it that is important.

Schaef has some valuable insights about romantic addiction. She says that more and more people are using sex and romance as a way of getting a fix, rather than as a means of relating. For many couples she sees in therapy, "getting enough sex" translates into avoiding tensions and feelings. They use lovemaking to keep from having to deal with themselves. In some cases the partners believe that making love is something they "deserve" and that their partner "owes" them. When a love addict gets a fix, it serves the same purpose as a drink or a drug, and the personality dynamics that develop are essentially the same.

Other Hidden Addictions: Food and Money

During the recent Presidential campaign, it was said in Washington circles that every time a Republican got into trouble, it was over money. Every time a Democrat did, it involved sex. Our preoccupation with food, money, and sex could well be characterized as "consuming passions." We live in a society that supports the accumulation of "more." It seems almost un-American to question whether our desire for more food, more money, and more sex might not be destructive. It will further help us understand love addiction to take a short detour into the world of food and wealth.

Judi Hollis, in her book *Fat Is a Family Affair*, makes some interesting observations about addictive relationships to food, addictions in general, and the relationship between food addiction and love addiction.[11]

Hollis says that addicts feel bad when they don't have their needed object, but they don't feel good when they do have it. Whether it's food, drugs, wealth, or love, there is a feeling of real discomfort if we don't have it. We become preoccupied with getting it, and yet we never feel fulfilled once we've gotten it.

Hollis makes clear the addictive pattern of dishonesty. To win love and admiration, addicts acquire an "as if" personality. They become what others need and want and lose their sense of self. When the authentic person inside us cries out to be heard, the addict within us may drown out the cries with food. Recovery from an eating disorder, as with any other addiction, requires a journey to find the real self.[12]

Hollis might have been talking about love addiction when she describes eating as a means of running away from others. She says that eating is a substitute for true intimacy and risk. The addict tries to get nurturance without making himself or herself vulnerable. Food, like other addictive substances or experiences, allows us to feel good without opening ourselves to fear and pain. People are never quite predictable or dependable; people sometimes expect too much of us. Refusing to risk the pain of separateness from others, of having their neediness not responded to, addicts choose the controlled security of food or some other "quick fix" that promises to "be there" for them.

Addiction to food, though still often hidden, has become the focus of increasing attention and concern among professionals and the general public. In our very materialistic society, however, few people recognize that the accumulation of money beyond what a person can ever use can become just as addictive and destructive as the accumulation of fat.

I would also suggest that there are many similarities between wealth addiction and addiction to romance. Many people who are addicted to one are addicted to the other, and since these addicts are often among the best and the brightest of our society, the destruction they cause goes unheeded.

66

I read recently about ten Wall Street executives who made more than $68 million each in 1986. The number-one moneymaker made $125 million in that year. Think about it: this man made $2.4 million a week, $480,000 a day, $60,000 an hour. Is this healthy activity or addictive acquisition?

Phillip Slater offers a brilliant analysis of this trend in his book *Wealth Addiction.*[13] A man and woman sit at home feeling proud of their ability to accumulate some extra money. They leaf through one of many colorful catalogues looking for something to buy. Having told themselves that they "need money," they must now consult a book to discover what they need the money for. We have become a nation of consumers who are constantly "going shopping," without a clear goal in mind. When that happens means and ends become reversed. Instead of acquiring money to help us get something we need, we buy something we don't need to help us spend the money we have acquired.

The confusion leads to addiction. When spending becomes separated from the satisfaction of basic needs, there is no natural satisfying conclusion. When I buy a watch in order to keep track of time, once I have a good watch I am satisfied and stop shopping. But what happens when I have amassed more money than I need? There's no satisfaction when I get "it" because I didn't need "it" to begin with. Rather than stopping and tuning into ourselves to find out what, if anything, we really want, in our anxiety we go out and buy something else.

We become a buying system that is out of control. The more we buy, the more we want to buy. Yet buying doesn't satisfy our inner needs, so we buy more, thinking that the problem is that we don't have enough. If you substitute "love" for "buying," you will see that the process of love addiction is identical.

Normally a thermostat works on the concept of "negative feedback." In the winter, when the temperature drops below a certain level, the thermostat causes the heat to turn on. When the heat rises and reaches a certain level, the heat turns off. A "positive feedback" loop would be created if the heat, reaching a certain temperature, sent a message to the thermostat to "turn on more heat." The hotter it would get, the more often the message would

67

be sent to "turn on more heat." Eventually the system would break down. Remember Janis Joplin's lament, "Too much ain't enough"? That's a positive feedback loop. It's also an addictive loop.

We see that at its core love addiction, like wealth addiction, can never be satisfied. We drive ourselves for "more"—more romance, more food, more alcohol, more money. If this description fits you, it may be time to consider that you may be addicted. If this description fits someone you love, it may be that you are a coaddict. People who find themselves in close, intimate contact with an addict suffer their own kind of hell. The following chapter focuses on coaddicts.

3. ARE YOU IN LOVE WITH A LOVE ADDICT?

"I Should Be a Better Lover"

It was Julia's first session and she was obviously nervous and disturbed. "My relationship with Paul is driving me crazy. We seem to fight all the time. We've been together for eight years," she said with an exasperated frown on her face. "It was so beautiful when we met. We traveled all over the world. Paul works for a large bank in New York which does business throughout Europe and South America and we were like two love birds playing wherever we went." Her eyes glistened as she looked off into space, recalling their recent life together. "Now we're at each other's throats all the time. We fight about everything, but mostly about the kids."

As the story unfolded, Julia, an attractive and stylishly dressed woman in her early fifties, told me that both she and Paul had sons from previous marriages. The boys were now in their early twenties and living in the area. Her son was attending a local college and Paul's was taking a semester off from a college he attended in the East and working with his dad. According to her, Paul was always shouting at her son, Donald, when he visited. "He's so damned demanding. If Donald isn't studying as much as he thinks he should, Paul gets down on him.''

Julia's deeper anger started coming to the surface as she described Paul's son, Robert. "Robert is such a slob. He's always leaving things around the house when he comes over and I'm expected to pick them up. And the kitchen! My God, whenever he's been in there it's like a cyclone went through. There's milk all over the counter. If something spills on the floor it stays there and your shoes stick to the floor when you walk in.''

I had a number of sessions with Julia and Paul together and a number with each separately. In the joint sessions they would constantly interrupt each other and became so angry they could barely stay in the same room together. "You don't listen to me!" "You don't care about me!" Though it was obvious to me that the anger had more to do with their own relationship than it did with their respective children, neither seemed able or willing to focus on how things were between them.

They seemed on the brink of separating, but both had been married previously and had had a number of serious relationships. They said they were willing to "hang in there" a little longer to see if we could get to the bottom of their difficulties. Julia and Paul had never had any serious bouts of physical violence, but had grabbed and slapped each other on a number of occasions; their emotional violence was obviously wearing them down. I thought it would be just a matter of time before one of them gave a clue to what was eating at them, and I hoped they could keep from destroying each other until we could get to it.

The break came after Julia missed an appointment. When she rescheduled the next week, she said she had been to the doctor. "I've got a vaginal infection and my doctor says I'm likely to have gotten it as a result of having sex." Julia looked down at her beautifully manicured nails as she continued hesitantly. "I was so embarrassed. My doctor gave me some medication and told me to see that everyone I've slept with recently got checked. I haven't slept with anyone but Paul!"

At the mention of Paul her anger rekindled. "I can't believe he did this to me!" Julia sat upright now as if she were getting ready for a fight. She seemed more sure of herself as she told me about the first year that she and Paul had spent together. "After we stopped traveling we bought a house and settled in. He still traveled a lot and I spent a lot of time with my painting. Paul would be gone two or three days at a time and when he got home, we'd make love a lot. I really missed him, but if I kept busy it was okay. He would always tell me where he was staying, in case of an emergency, but I never felt he really wanted me to interrupt his work, so I never called."

Julia suddenly seemed more frightened than angry as she continued. "Well, on one of his trips some papers came in the mail that he needed to sign immediately and I thought I'd better call him. I called the hotel where he was staying.

"It was so strange," she said shaking her head. "The desk clerk told me no one by that name was registered. I told him that was impossible. I gave the company name, but he had no record of that either. . . . I kind of lost control. I don't know why, I just got panicked. I started screaming at the poor guy. I finally hung up and burst into tears. I was sure something terrible had happened to Paul. The only thing that helped me get through the next day was support from my son and talking to my sister.

"When he came back home, I had calmed down some. I told him I had called the hotel and they said he wasn't registered there. He paused for a moment, then laughed and told me this elaborate story about a client coming in from out of town who was staying at another hotel. He said he decided to change hotels so he could stay closer to the client and make it easier to do business. He apologized for not calling me. I still wasn't sure, but he was so convincing. I felt so foolish," Julia said looking down in her lap. "I'm just being a typical hysterical woman, I thought. No wonder Paul gets mad at me. We both seemed to be extra considerate of each other over the next few weeks. Our love life was great, until I got a vaginal infection and we had to stop while the medication took effect."

The panic returned as Julia continued with her story. "Two months later, I was cleaning out the pockets of one of Paul's suits before taking it to the cleaner and I found a card with the name

71

of a hotel and a woman's name written on it. I couldn't believe it, but I knew I had to find out. I called the hotel and said I was Paul's wife and had lost our receipt and needed it for tax purposes. He confirmed that 'Mr. and Mrs.' had indeed been registered the two nights he was away.

"I confronted him and he finally admitted he had seen a woman. He told me it was the only time it had ever happened. He said he was lonely for me and met this woman on the plane flying into New York. He cried and I cried and he swore it would never happen again.

"I just wanted things to be good between us. I needed to be needed and I was in love with him. I put all my anger on the 'woman' who seduced him and on myself. I told myself I'm too clingy, I should be a better lover."

The life seemed to drain out of Julia as she concluded her story. "Now I've got an infection again and wonder if he's been sleeping around. I don't know what to believe. I don't know if I'm being a blind fool or if I'm paranoid. Can you help me sort it out?"

Giving It All Up for Love

Julia's story is typical of people who fall in love with love addicts. They share with the addicts themselves a deep feeling of insecurity. While the addict becomes blinded by his addiction, the person in love with the addict—the co-addict—becomes blind to the behavior of the addict. Julia became hooked on Paul. Gradually she began to distort more and more of her experience in order to "keep things smooth" between them. However, the more she tried to keep things under control, the more they got out of hand.

As Julia said, "I thought I had finally found a man who was special, who loved only me. If I could just make him happy, I believed, my life would be complete. As time went on I got more and more frantic. I couldn't bear to think of my life without him. I was sure I would die if he ever left me."

The more Julia would try to make it "right," the more "wrong" things became. We've seen that this process is at the core of addictions, whether the addiction is to love itself or to someone who is a love addict.

We can get a clearer picture of how co-addiction works through the following analogy. Let's imagine that a woman lives in the country a good distance from people. In the area where she lives there are two springs. In one spring the water contains quite a large quantity of copper, but no other elements. The second spring contains calcium and a variety of other trace elements that are essential to human life.

The woman is aware of the copper in the first spring. She can taste it. It has a satisfying taste, bringing up memories of her childhood. There is something comforting and familiar about the first spring.

Occasionally wandering travelers stop at the springs to refresh themselves. They seem to have an equal preference for both springs, but the woman begins to fear that the first spring may run dry and she decides to move closer to it to protect her supply. She rarely goes to the second spring and her body begins to feel the lack of the elements it contains.

Blinded by her addictive belief that she needs copper, she becomes convinced that her weakness and disagreeable symptoms are a result of not getting enough copper-filled water. She starts drinking twice as much of it as before and now begins to experience symptoms of a copper overdose, as well as continuing to have deficiency symptoms because of the lack of other needed elements in her life. As time goes on and her addictive attachment to the first spring increases, she cuts herself off more completely from other sources of refreshment.

In most addictions, and co-addiction in particular, the primary harm comes not from the direct effects of the addictive relationship, but from what one gives up as the addiction progresses. Most heroin addicts, for instance, suffer more from the fact that they don't eat well or take care of their health than from the harmful effects of the heroin itself. Most co-addicts suffer as they cut themselves off from friends, from the activities that are meaningful to them, and ultimately from their own beliefs about themselves and their values.

73

And as they become more deprived in other areas of their life, they cling even more closely to their addict lover.

As I worked more with Julia the parallel pattern of decreased involvement in other things and increased dependence on Paul became evident. "When we first met physical contact was a very important part of our life. We made love a lot and enjoyed it. But we also did a lot of other things, both together and apart. I had my friends and my art and Paul had his work." Julia shook her head in confusion as she continued. "I don't really know how it happened, but gradually I started seeing my friends less and less often. Paul didn't really like them. He used to kid me about how 'artsy fartsy' they were. He never pressured me, or ever suggested I not see them, but gradually things just cooled off with them.

"I know after a while I began to feel guilty that it had been so long since I'd had contact with them. That made it even harder to call. And my own art work seemed to become less important to me. I don't know—after a while I kind of lost confidence in myself.

"I began to put more and more time into my appearance. I wanted to be sexy and attractive for him. I didn't mind giving up other things because I cared so much for him and wanted to please him. When he began to bring home pornographic books and magazines, at first I was uncomfortable. But he insisted it would liven up our love life, and I thought, 'What the hell, I'll try anything once.'

"Well, he wanted to do things that I . . ." Julia became flustered and embarrassed as she continued. "You know, they seemed kind of way-out. But I went along. I thought I would start enjoying them if I loosened up. He was always telling me I needed to loosen up, that I was a 'Miss Goody Two-shoes,' and I thought he was right.

"The things we did weren't really that upsetting to me. I like sex as much as anyone. But what started getting to me was that he would want me to be available at a moment's notice. He would come home late after a meeting and begin fondling me at the front door. At first I was flattered that he was so turned on to me. But later it felt like pressure. He would wake me up in the middle of the night to make love or want to make love all night. He introduced me to cocaine, which he said would make me feel sexy, but all it did was make me feel jittery and nervous. That's when the fights about the children began."

Julia sat up with a start. "I never really connected the two before." It took her some time to begin to understand her own pattern and to see that in fact it had gone on with other men in her life. She began to see that her inability to say no to men was related to her fear of losing a relationship she had become more and more dependent upon. The loneliness and isolation that prompted her to try even harder to "make him happy" were familiar old patterns. Finally, she was able to see that her own needs had never been seen as important. From the time she was a child she had learned to put other people's needs ahead of her own. Whenever there was a conflict, she assumed automatically that it must be she who had done something wrong. As Julia began to see the part she played in the conflict with Paul and to see that the fights about the children really were covering over the more basic addictive style of the relationship, she was able to seek out the support she needed to make changes. I encouraged her to join a 12-step program for spouses of addicted people.

His Secret Life

Julia said she did not want me to tell Paul what she had revealed to me. She said she was afraid he would leave her if he knew. I told her I would respect her wishes. I told her that the sexually addicted man is afraid to let others know about his addiction. But another side of him, the healthy side, wants desperately to let someone in and share his secrets. That was true of Paul. As time went on, he began to reveal more about his secret sexual and romantic life.

"I thought I would die when Julia found out about the affair I was having," he said. He spoke with an air of bravado. "I tried to devise a story on the spot that made sense, but it was obvious that she had caught me. When I told her it would never happen again I believed it. Just the thought of losing her . . ." His voice trailed off and a flash of fear seemed to cross his face, but he quickly covered it and went on with some anger.

"You know, you couldn't really blame me for having the affair. I was under a lot of pressure at work and being away from Julia was tough on me. I hadn't really planned that it would happen. I'd always been attracted to the woman. She was the secretary to the president of one of the firms I visited. When I knew I was coming into town I called and asked if she wanted to have dinner. One thing led to another—you know—and we decided to spend the night together."

Two things became apparent when Paul told the story. One was that he tended to blame others for the affair. It was caused by the pressures, or the circumstances, never his own desire. The other was that even in "coming clean" to Julia, he had apparently not told her the whole truth. He had told her it was a woman he had just met on the plane; he was telling me it was someone he had already known and found attractive and that he had set up the date in advance.

I've found that the fear of telling the truth is so strong for love addicts that they will often lie, even when being honest would be easier. Sometimes they are so good at lying to themselves that they aren't even conscious their stories aren't convincing.

One of the major difficulties for a person in love with a love addict is to know what is really true. Until the whole truth is known, the relationship is based on a shaky foundation. Often the truth is revealed slowly, if at all. It's like pulling away the layers of an onion. There seems always to be one more layer. Yet it is critical to get to the heart of the matter, if there is to be any hope for the relationship.

Over many months of working with Paul, more and more of the truth was revealed. He told me that he had in fact had many affairs. These had been going on before the marriage as well as afterward. They usually occurred while he was away on business trips. "I've always loved the ladies," he revealed with a little less of his earlier bravado. "Sometimes I feel I can't stay away even when I want to."

As time went on he talked more about the compulsive nature of

76

his involvements with women. "Every time I take a plane to another city, I find myself flirting with one of the stewardesses. I always felt fine about it. Just clean manly fun." He paused and looked down at his manicured fingers. "But I've begun to notice that even when I've got work to do, when I *need* to get some work done on the plane, I can't seem to concentrate. It's like the women have some power over me."

During another session Paul revealed more of his fear about the romantic behavior interfering with his work. "After I've met with the men and discussed our business over dinner, they excuse themselves and return to their wives or go to their rooms. I do the same. But I can't stay in my room. I get restless and anxious. I always go find a bar in another area, and always go looking for women. Sometimes I pick someone up and we make love together. More often I just sit and fantasize. Either way, I find that I'm blitzed the next day and have real difficulty making it in for my morning appointments."

This is characteristic of love addicts. Their romantic preoccupations and behavior begin to interfere more and more directly in their lives. It isn't just making love that draws them, but the excitement of meeting someone new. They find that they increasingly move beyond limits that they have set for themselves.

"I've always made it a policy," Paul said as he leaned forward in his chair, "never to get involved with women I work with. But damn, I don't know how it happened. I've become involved with one of the female executives in our Chicago branch. It's strictly against company policy and it would cause real problems if it were ever discovered, but I can't seem to do anything about it."

As Paul's addictive behavior got more and more out of control, his secret life became more difficult to hide. Little bits of it began to intrude into his work and home life. Often those who are romantically involved with love addicts are the first to see the early warning signs. However, their own needs for security keep them from allowing themselves to see the truth. There are usually inklings that something isn't quite right with the relationship even from the very beginning, but the addict and the co-addict collude to deny the problem.

77

Early Warning Signals

As Julia continued her work in therapy and in her 12-step group, she started to remember some of these early warning signs that she had failed to acknowledge in the past.

"I think back now and there were signs that I overlooked. When I first met Paul he was engaged to marry a woman who I knew slightly. We had met at a cocktail party and he seemed very attracted to me. There was something electric between us. We both felt it." She paused and her face flushed as she recalled their first meeting. "Even though he had come to the party with his fiancée, he and I managed to get off alone together on the terrace. It was very romantic. He kissed me, gently at first, then more and more passionately. I think we would have made love right out in the open if someone hadn't come out.

"In the weeks that followed, he would drop in unexpectedly at work. I was working in a gallery then and the sight of him would send shivers up my spine. I would get off early and we'd head for my apartment. He was still living with his fiancée and I don't know what he told her. I just felt like I was the most desirable person in the world if he would give up so much to be with me. It never occurred to me to question how easy it seemed for Paul to make the switch from her to me.

"He broke his engagement and we decided to move in together the next month. We went to Las Vegas to celebrate. We went to one of those extravaganzas with hundreds of scantily clad women, you know the kind. I expected that Paul would get all excited looking at the women and then we'd go back to our room and make love. All evening he kept glancing over at a woman sitting at the next table. At times I felt like I wasn't even there. He would quickly come back from his reverie when we'd talk, but he didn't seem really with me. He seemed detached.

"After the show I went back to the room to get ready and Paul said he wanted to buy a newspaper and would be back shortly. He didn't come back for hours and when he did he was drunk. He said he had met an old college buddy and they had gone to the bar for a few drinks. I was crying by then and when I questioned him more, he got really nasty and started yelling at me."

She was sobbing deeply now, but at the same time seemed to be holding back her pain, as if she had no right to feel hurt.

"He was extremely loving the next day. He took me out and we had a wonderful time. I just didn't want to think about the night before and I was just glad everything was back to normal. I guess I just didn't want to see the truth. Paul had a thing for women all along. I kept thinking that I could make him love only me. If I could just be more attractive and make our lives so inviting, he would forget about anyone else."

The Male Co-addict

For those who are in love with love addicts, life becomes a series of fights and reconciliations. You never feel quite grounded, as though the earth is always shifting under your feet. Your one desire is to hold on to the person of your dreams. But the more you try to be "everything" to your partner, the more he or she seems to slip away. Although it is true that most love addicts are male and most co-addicts female, addiction does not discriminate between the sexes. Men are just as capable of loving someone whose life has become unmanageable because of romantic activities as are women.

Alan was a case in point. He had come to see me because he was afraid of losing his wife. A nice-looking man in his mid-thirties, he seemed nervous, almost skittish, as though he were afraid something might jump out at him any minute.

"We've been married seven years and have three beautiful kids," Alan said. "But in the last few years things haven't been good between us. I feel like it's mostly my fault. I've been spending more and more time at work and Rita says she never sees me anymore." Alan looked as if he were about to cry as he fumbled for the words to continue. "I'm really confused. I don't know what's going on, but I feel down. There are times I just want Rita to hold me and tell me she loves me. But I hate myself for feeling so weak. I'm afraid if I really let myself go, I'd just want to curl up in her arms and never come out again." Alan's face showed a mixture of longing and terror at the thought of "letting go." "When I'm at work, at least I feel like a man."

He seemed to be having difficulty talking about the present and we shifted to talking about their past. "We met when we were in college in North Carolina. Rita was a junior and I was a senior. I first saw her at a scholarship reception and asked her out for coffee afterwards. She was young and vivacious and a little bit crazy. I liked her spunk. I was getting ready to go to law school the next year and it seemed like all I ever did was study.

"Rita seemed like a breath of fresh air. She was obviously intelligent, but she didn't take life too seriously. We started to see each other every day and would spend hours walking on the beach and talking about life." Alan's mood seemed to lift as he talked about his time with Rita in college. "I was kind of straitlaced and conservative. She would grab my hand, and out of the blue, start screaming at the top of her lungs and begin running along the sand, pulling me after her. I was embarrassed, but I loved it. I had never known anyone who was such a free spirit.

"She was a free spirit in love as well. I had never gone 'all the way' with a girl. I don't know why, really. I know I was always afraid of getting a girl pregnant and I remember my mother telling me that if I really loved a girl, I'd take care of her. It seemed I was more concerned about protecting the girls' virginity than they were. With Rita, it was different. She was taking birth-control pills, in order to control her periods she said. I looked at her with disbelief.

" 'No, really,' Rita said, 'I never knew I was taking birth-control pills until my girlfriend told me. I thought they were pills to help control my periods. I always had such an unpredictable cycle and such heavy flow, the pills seemed to help.'

"It was clear, though, once she did find out that the pills could be used to protect against unwanted pregnancy, she wasted no time exploring the world of sexual freedom. She seemed as uninhibited about sex as she was about running on the beach. I tried to match her experience. After all, I was the senior and she was the junior. I implied that I had had much more experience sexually than I actually had. I wanted to impress her and I couldn't let her know that I was still a virgin when we met. I had read a lot about sex so I figured I could fake it pretty well.

"I remember the first time we made love. I was terrified. We snuck out of the dorms on a warm spring night and went down to a park. All I could think about was that someone was going to see us and I would be caught with my pants down, so to speak. She pretty much had to direct things. I was just glad I could keep my erection. It wasn't much fun for me, and I'm sure it wasn't that great for her either. But she told me what a wonderful lover I was and I wanted to believe her.

"She stayed with one of her girlfriends that summer and we dated. I thought I was the only one in her life, but she made it clear that she needed her space and was dating other guys, though she kept telling me I was her special man. I was a bit uncomfortable with the arrangement. I didn't feel like seeing anyone else, but I wanted her to be happy and I told her it was fine with me that she see other guys.

"When we returned to school in the fall, she told me she didn't want to see me anymore. I was crushed." Tears filled his eyes as he choked back his feelings. "I still remember it like it was yesterday. It's the same way I'm feeling now—like I've been kicked. I felt hurt and alone and I kept asking her, 'Why, tell me why you don't want to see me?' She just said, 'Because I don't love you anymore.' It just didn't seem possible. I couldn't accept that love could come and go so easily.

"For days I just lay in bed. I couldn't do my schoolwork and I didn't want to see any of my friends. I barely ate anything at all, usually only when a friend brought something by. After about a week I decided I'd better get on with my life. I told myself the hell with her, I don't need her, and started dating again." Alan seemed almost frenzied as he continued. "I started going out with anyone and everyone. I had a date with a different girl each night of the week. I felt like I had something to prove, but I didn't know what it was and it really didn't make me happy. I never had sex with any of the girls I dated. In some way I guess I was hoping that if I didn't 'betray' Rita, maybe she would come back to me.

81

"I remember one really humiliating day talking to Rita's best friend. I cried and begged her to help me get her back. I said I couldn't live without her and I'd do anything to have her. She just held my hand and told me to forget her.

"I just couldn't let her go. I decided I would try one more time to get her back. I took the prettiest girl I could find to a dance where I knew Rita would be present. We danced and held each other close and I did everything I could to make her jealous.

"Well, I guess it worked," Alan said with a sad but triumphant voice. "The next week she called me up and wanted to get together for coffee. As soon as we saw each other we practically leaped into each other's arms. It was like we had never been apart. The only thing she asked was that we never talk about what we'd each been doing during the time we were separate. I remember feeling a little uneasy. I hadn't done anything I wouldn't want her to know about. I wondered what she'd done. But I pushed the whole thing out of my mind. I was so glad to get her back and I didn't really care what was being left unsaid."

"I Couldn't Give Her Enough"

Those who are in love with love addicts continually override the inner doubts that tell them something is wrong. They are so happy to feel wanted and cared for, they are willing to push any negative thoughts under the rug. The doubts often come back to haunt them, however.

Over the next few sessions Alan talked about his graduation, going on to law school, his marriage to Rita, and the birth of their children. He began to unearth some of the doubts that he had buried so long ago. "Just before we got married Rita told me about a brief affair she had had while I was out of town. She assured me it didn't mean anything. I remember a thought crossing my mind: I can't trust this woman, I ought to call this off. The thought was short-lived and the fear of losing her just intensified my desire to get married quickly, so I'd know I had her. I thought marriage would put to rest any desire she had for other men. I told myself

82

she was just young and crazy and as soon as she settled down things would be fine."

Alan sighed and the sad, scared look returned as he continued with his story. "Things were great for the first few years. We were both madly in love. We didn't have much money while I was in school. I had a scholarship that paid pretty well and Rita worked part-time. When we had time to go out it was always a treat. We made love a lot, which didn't cost any money. It always amazed me how free she seemed to be. She was always wanting to try out new things. She'd come home with a new oil or a magazine. She'd want me to make up fantasies about making love with other people.

"The thought of making love with anyone else terrified me. I was sure if she ever got connected with anyone else again, she would leave me. But I wanted to please her and I went along with all her fantasy ideas. I even took the lead eventually. I guess I thought if I could be in charge of what we did, at least I could control things.

"Besides, it was the time of the sexual revolution. Everyone was reading novels like Robert Rimmer's *The Harrad Experiment,* about an experimental college that promoted sexual experience as part of their curriculum. Many of our married friends were reading George and Nena O'Neill's *Open Marriage.* I remember thinking that the traditional 'closed marriage' was doomed to failure. It was based on fear and ownership of your partner. I thought about my parents' marriage. It was closed and rigid and unsatisfying. They divorced when I was eleven. I didn't know if 'open marriage' would work, but I felt I had to do something—anything—to hold on to Rita.

"We talked for hours about who we were attracted to among our friends. We speculated on who was sleeping with whom. It was actually kind of exciting. Usually after a session of discussing the pros—somehow we never got around to discussing the cons—of open marriage, we would get all turned on to each other and make mad, passionate love. I hoped the talk would just go on forever. It seemed like a nice way to keep things exciting, but never have to risk acting on the feelings."

Romantic addiction, however, doesn't remain static. The behaviors don't give us the satisfactions we crave and we seek ever more

83

exciting experiences to give us what we feel we lack. The person in love with the love addict tries harder and harder to please and hold on to the addict. The addict wants ever more exciting intrigues.

Alan seemed to be getting tense as he continued. "Rita went along with my idea to have an old buddy from law school stay with us while he was getting himself established in the area. Rob and I had been friends all through school. She and Rob weren't close but they seemed to enjoy each other when we would meet at lectures or parties.

"It was great having him stay with us. He was like the brother I never had and it seemed to get Rita and me off all the talk about sexual liberation. While he was there we seemed to be like brothers and sister, three little kids enjoying each other and playing. As an only child, I had missed that feeling of connection. The weeks moved quickly as we worked and played and ate together.

"We decided to take a vacation together at Lake Tahoe. We got two rooms with a connecting bathroom. We'd swim and boat during the day, eat and gamble at night. One evening after returning to our room for drinks we got into one of our philosophical discussions about open marriage. I quipped that if 'you two ever get interested in each other, I hope you'll tell me.' It was great to feel we could talk about sex and what *others* might do." Tears welled up in his eyes. "But my world shattered in a million pieces when Rita smiled and said 'We're interested in each other.' I felt like I'd been kicked in the balls, but I smiled and swallowed hard and said 'Let's talk about it.'

"They were romantically attracted to each other, they said, and wanted to make love, but didn't want to have it threaten anything between us. I felt sick inside. I kept thinking if I tell them no, that's not what I want, I'll lose her. If I let them go ahead she'll probably choose him over me and I'll still lose her."

Alan began to cry softly now. "They seemed so concerned about me, wanting me to decide what was best. I just couldn't say no. We agreed that they would go into Rob's room and I would stay in ours. When they were done Rita would come back to me.

"It seemed like an eternity of waiting. I was sure they would have a quick physical encounter, Rita would return and say he was nice, but not at all what she was used to, and we would make love for the rest of the night. As the time rolled on, I could hear them from the next room. I wanted to run away. The sounds of their lovemaking were driving me crazy. But I'd told myself I would wait. How would I ever know if she was coming back unless I waited? I had to prove I was strong and that she would come back to me. Finally, I couldn't stand it anymore and burst into their room, sobbing. They stopped and brought me into their bed. I so much wanted to feel their care and warmth, but I realized I was in the middle of their love nest and I felt sick."

As I sat listening to Alan and feeling his pain, I realized the depth to which those who are in love with love addicts will go in order to hold on to them. I couldn't imagine a more diabolical form of self-torture.

"I've never told anyone else the story," Alan concluded. "I feel relieved in a way. Things went downhill from there. Once the door was open for Rita to sleep with others she just couldn't seem to stop. Or she didn't want to. Whenever I would try to talk to her about my hurt or pain, she would say that I started it. 'You're the one who talked about open marriage. You're the one who invited Rob to stay with us. You're the one who said that a closed marriage was unhealthy.' Her arguments seemed to make sense to my 'liberated' mind. I always felt guilty that I wasn't giving her enough and I always felt like I had to go along.

"I want the marriage to work. I know Rita needs her freedom and I want to give it to her, but the jealousy is killing me. Every time she's out now, I fantasize about who she's with. I feel like I'm being pulled apart. I want to just forget who she's with, but I can't seem to let it alone. What can I do to change?"

A Look at Love

If you are in love with a love addict, whether you are male or female, there are probably a number of things you have in common with both Alan and Julia. If asked why you stay in a relationship that is obviously causing so much pain, the answer you would probably give is "Because I love him/her." We feel there is something special about the person, a certain kind of "magic" that lights up our lives. At other times we feel that this can't be love. Love is supposed to be kind and gentle; what we feel is pain. Whether we're sure that what we feel is true love or whether we feel we are experiencing some kind of insanity, we do believe that if things are not going the way we want them, it must be our fault and we must do the changing in the relationship.

The reality of "love" in this situation is that it is a mixture of real love and addictive love. The addictive love grows out of control like a cancer, and begins to choke out the real love in the relationship. Starved for love, the co-addict tries even harder to "make things work," but is in the grip of a deadly compulsion. The more he or she struggles to make things right, the greater the despair.

The goal of understanding isn't so you can get rid of this person or throw away the love; that would be like throwing the baby out with the bathwater. The hope is that by understanding the difference between addictive love and real love, you can begin to withdraw energy from the addictive aspects and put it into building up the real love. Ultimately, whether you stay with the person or decide to leave, it will be a free choice, not a compulsion. It will be a choice made as a result of love, not addiction.

The first step in the recovery process is being able to acknowledge that there is something unhealthy about the way you love. Trying harder to love better won't work, since more of the same is simply more of an unhealthy process. In fact, the first characteristic of addictive love is that it requires so much effort. We feel we must "work" at our relationships. But when they become all work and no play, something is wrong.

Remember what it was like when things were really going well? Do you remember how easily love seemed to flow? Think now about how hard you are trying, how much effort and thought goes into making the relationship work.

The second characteristic of addictive love is its basis in fear. We're never sure if the other person really loves us. When we're at a party or out socially, we wonder whether we are attractive enough or sexy enough or entertaining enough to be loved. Love

86

lives under a cloud, and the cloud is fear, fear that we will be abandoned.

The third characteristic of addictive love is its neediness. Addictive love is always insecure. It always cries out for more. When we say "I love him," our love is dominated by our need. We often try to hide our neediness, fearing that if our partner knew how dependent we felt, how needy we were, he or she would love us less. We're often most aware of the needy quality of our love when we become afraid of losing our partner. This can happen in response to a seemingly insignificant event like our partner being late getting home. As the minutes go by, we may get worried, then panicked, sure the person has been killed in an accident. We picture ourselves shriveling and dying without our love to sustain us.

The fourth characteristic of addictive love is its blindness. We are blind to behaviors of our partner that threaten our secure view of the relationship. We rationalize—"He had a rough day," "She's just finding her freedom"—in order to convince ourselves that our partner's behavior is really acceptable when in fact it is hurtful and humiliating to us. We blind ourselves to the lies and half-truths that demonstrate our partner's irresponsible romantic behavior. We tell ourselves that we trust them, when in fact we are telling ourselves that we are too afraid to know the truth.

The fifth characteristic of addictive love is its consuming quality. We feel overwhelmed by love, we lose ourselves in it. Our love becomes more and more restrictive. We cut ourselves off from friends we care about, from activities that we once treasured, and from loving ourselves. Our overriding concern is loving the other person. We become preoccupied and obsessed, often neglecting our children, friends, parents, coworkers, and ourselves, because we must be increasingly available to our partner. Yet the more we give, the more our addict lover seems to demand of us. We become increasingly terrified that we will fall short. Ultimately, we become willing to sacrifice our lives to feed our addictive love. What began as love finally becomes its opposite; we embrace death.

I don't use these words—fear, neediness, blindness, death—melodramatically. Those who are in love with a love addict know deep in their hearts that they are actually on a path that leads to destruction. Experts in the field of addictions now know that co-addicts often die sooner than the addicts themselves.

Let's look at the addict again. The addict has become hooked on certain romantic practices. Because of the nature of these activities and the stigma attached to them, it is not surprising that they want to hide their behavior and that those in love with them do not want to see what is going on. Love addicts always lead secret lives. The secrets may be in their fantasies, in their behavior, or both. Yet they desperately want to be cared for and accepted for who they are, not who they pretend to be.

The person in love with the addict will often be the first to glimpse the secret life, noticing alibis and inconsistencies in stories, receipts found in coats, the stash of porno magazines. Addicts want to hide because they are ashamed of what they do. They also want more than anything else to come out and be seen.

Health and survival for the addict and the person in love with the addict depend upon the truth being revealed. The longer we allow our fear and denial to keep us locked into old patterns, the more destructive the behavior will become. Love addicts want help, just like alcoholics and drug addicts. Since the person in love with the addict is often the first person in a position to see clues clearly enough, he or she is in a position to help.

If you are wondering whether the person you are with is a love addict, you may want to turn to the self-help questionnaire on pages 198–203 of this book. Answer the questions *as if* you were your partner and could be totally honest about your behavior. If you say to yourself, "I just don't know how my partner would answer this question," let yourself *imagine* the answer. The purpose isn't to get the goods on your partner, it's to help you break through your own veil of denial and be able to see clearly the reality of his or her addiction. This won't happen all at once. If you can allow yourself to trust that the truth will in fact set you free, you can begin to see your partner as he or she really is.

Your partner may be a love addict. If that's the situation, it doesn't mean they are perverted, crazy, or bad. It does mean he or she needs help. This book is meant to help you both know whether love addictions are harming your relationship and to help you find the guidance you need.

Characteristics of a Co-addict

Now let's look at you. In your need to be needed, you have focused more and more of your attention and energy on your partner. When you've looked at yourself it has been with the desire to answer such questions as "What can I do better?" and "How can I change myself in order to make my partner happier?"

To be able to answer the question "Am I in love with a love addict?" you must be willing to look honestly at yourself in ways that are new to you. You need to recognize that in some ways it is just as difficult for you to see yourself clearly as it is for your partner.

When you do look honestly at yourself you will find that you are not in this relationship by accident. You will see certain patterns in your life that go back to childhood. You will see that you share many of the characteristics of the addict. You will also see that co-addiction has many unique characteristics as well. What follows are some of the ways those who are in love with addicts characterize themselves. Let yourself be open to any of these statements that may be true for you:

1. I came from a family in which my emotional needs weren't met. I often felt insecure and unsure about my lovability. I thought I had to earn my parents' love through good deeds.

2. I've always been attracted to the care-giving role. I felt responsible for "fixing things" in my family. As an adult, I seem to attract people who need help. I love to feel needed.

3. I never gave up my hope that somehow I could get love if I could find the right person to whom I could give love. I tend to be attracted to emotionally unavailable people who I keep hoping I can change by loving them like they've never been loved before.

4. My worst fear is of being abandoned. Fearful of being alone, I spend a lot of my energy finding a partner. Once in a relationship I do whatever I can to be sure I am not abandoned, to keep things smooth and prevent making waves.

89

5. I often put my own needs on hold in order to take care of someone else. Meeting the needs of someone I love often overshadows having my own needs met.

6. I find it much easier to do for others than to ask for help for myself. I definitely live the maxim "It is better to give than to receive."

7. I don't expect to be loved, but I need very much to be loved. I go out of my way to give. I am patient to a fault, and often give much more than I receive.

8. When someone I love wraps me up in their arms, I feel I'm in heaven. At times I want to cry out "Hold me, hold me, never let me go!"

9. When there is a conflict I often feel responsible and take the blame for any hurt I may have caused others. I'm always looking for ways to improve myself.

10. I have low self-esteem. I try to do more and do better so that I can be accepted by people. No matter how well others say I do or how complimentary they are to me, I can't quite believe them.

11. I've always felt conflicted about sex. I learned early that sex was something I should give in order to please another person. I'm not at all sure what I like in making love, apart from the pleasure I get pleasing the person I care about.

12. Because I feel insecure, I must control the other person. I do that by being helpful, available, and understanding. If I'm needed enough I protect myself against being left.

13. I have an active fantasy life about how good the relationship would be "if." I keep hoping my partner will change if I'm good enough. I sometimes get lost in the world of my imagination. How I would like it to be overshadows how it really is.

14. I often feel depressed and sad, and have a tendency to escape through the use of medications, food, drugs, or alcohol. I feel I'm not okay the way I am and need something to cover my uncomfortable feelings. Sometimes I think people would be better off without me.

15. I seem to get hooked on partners whose lives are chaotic and abusive. I tell myself I don't want that kind of person in my life, but they seem to gravitate toward me.

90

16. I find I am not attracted to stable, caring, healthy people. Sometimes I tell myself there aren't any "good" people out in the world. When I do meet someone nice, they often seem dull and boring. Being with them has no ups and downs; it's pointless and dull.

17. I have a feeling that focusing so much attention on my partner prevents me from looking inside at my own fears and problems.

If you have recognized yourself in any of the statements above, there is a good chance that you have some addictive characteristics. Like the addict, you may feel at first that you are "bad." But please remember that no one chooses to look for love in all the wrong places because they are evil or crazy. We do it because that's how we've learned to love. There *is* a better way, however, and you will find it as you continue to read.

4. COMING TOGETHER AND COMING APART: The Approach-Avoidance Dance

"The Thought of Settling Down Scares Me"

Sam called saying he had heard about my work. He indicated he didn't feel he had any major problems, that life was going pretty well for him, but he just felt that working with me might help his general well-being.

When he arrived for his first appointment, in fact, he looked like someone who enjoyed life. It was a warm summer day in Los Angeles and Sam was dressed in shorts. He wore running shoes without socks and it was obvious from his thin, muscular legs that he ran regularly. He was tall, blond, and good-looking, with a boyish smile that belied the fact that he had just turned forty.

His life seemed to match his appearance. "I'm a tennis instructor at a local health and fitness club," Sam began. He had a gentle voice with just a touch of a midwestern accent. "It's great. Most of the people who come to the club have money and really want to learn to play tennis. I love the game myself. Sometimes I can't believe I'm really being paid to do something I love so much and I seem to attract beautiful women." He smiled his boyish smile.

"When I'm not working I run every day and paint in my spare

time. I've sold a few of my pieces. They're mostly modern, abstract works based on American Indian art. Sometimes I think I'd like to be an artist full time and get out of the tennis business. But the pay there is excellent. I've been doing it for ten years and I'm really good at it.''

He talked about growing up on a ranch in the Midwest. He had little social life beyond the family. His dream then was to move to the big city and "party." He seemed to have achieved his dream. I assumed he was a freewheeling bachelor by the way he described all the beautiful women who were attracted to him, but after a number of weeks he talked about Kirsten.

"Kirsten is wonderful," he said with a gleam in his eye. "I really love her a lot. She's intelligent, creative, and fun to be with. We like the same things and we both enjoy the good life. We love to go to good restaurants." He paused and shook his head and smiled. "But we eat at home a lot. She's an incredible cook. She could open a restaurant if she wanted. She does do catering sometimes, in fact. But her real passion—would you believe this—is finance. She works at a bank and is a senior officer specializing in overseas investments."

I wondered if there was anything missing for Sam. I finally asked him directly. "Everything you've said so far about your life sounds great. It's a pleasure to talk with someone who isn't experiencing major crises like so many people these days. But no life is perfect. Are there any areas of *your* life that aren't working perfectly for you?''

There was a long silence as he looked up toward the ceiling. I wasn't sure if he was thinking whether he really had any problems or whether or not to tell me about them. When he did respond he seemed to lose some of his self-assurance.

"There are really two areas of my life that I'm concerned about at times. I'm not sure they're really problems. One is my use of marijuana and the other is my relationship with Kirsten.

"I smoke after work to relax. Most of the time I feel fine about it. I've accepted the fact that it's illegal and I'm very careful so I'm not worried about getting busted. Sometimes I smoke a lot. I kinda go overboard." Sam looked a little sheepish as he continued.

94

"It really doesn't cause problems, but I'm such a health nut I wonder about its effect on my lungs and when I do overdo it, I feel logy the next day.

"I guess my real concern, though, is with Kirsten and me. We've been together for three years and things are great, as I said, except lately she's talking about getting married and . . . I don't know if I'm scared or what. I've never been married before. I always thought I would be, but never seemed to meet the right person. She's everything I've ever wanted, but the thought of settling down scares me.

"We've talked about it before and what usually happens is that I begin to see things her way and feel it would be a good idea to get married. Then we get into a fight. I'm not ever sure whether she starts it or I do. But the result is that we get more distant. We've even broken up on a number of occasions, but as soon as we're apart I want her back."

As I listened to Sam I thought of many other couples I had worked with over the years and I thought about my own relationships. There often seemed to be this "approach-avoidance" dance. We want to get close and settle down, but there's something about intimacy that scares us and we withdraw, only to feel lonely and wanting to get close again.

In the following weeks Sam's issues became clearer and the first indications of love addiction were revealed.

"In some ways I feel like a perpetual adolescent," he said during one of our sessions. "I feel like I never really grew up. I'm still playing the games I played as a kid and I still find myself lusting over beautiful girls." He looked down at the floor, then up. His smile was gone. "I've never told this to anyone before, but a lot of the attraction of the job is that I see beautiful women all the time. I find myself fantasizing about making love with them. And before I met Kirsten that's what I did. It was like a big game. They seemed to want sex and I was ready to give it to them. Since I've been with her, I want to stop, but I don't feel I can.

"I've definitely cut down on how often I make love with other women, but I can't seem to stop completely. I'm not sure if I make love with other women to keep from getting close to Kirsten or whether I don't want to get too close to her so I can keep having a free, unrestricted love life. But I do know that I feel out of control. I tell myself no more, but the promise lasts only until the next pretty woman comes in for a lesson."

As Sam began to see the connection between the conflicts in his relationship with Kirsten and his romantic preoccupation with beautiful women, he began to gain a whole new perspective on his life.

The Love Triad

Love addiction, by its very nature, is not a solitary problem. We treat cancer or tuberculosis by focusing on the individual. But it makes no more sense to focus on the love addict alone than it does to consider impregnation as involving only the male or the female.

There is always a triangular relationship involved in love addiction. There is a real-world relationship that the addict wants to change to meet his or her needs and a fantasy-ideal relationship that the addict always pursues. As a result the addict is always caught in an approach-avoidance dance. "I want you, but I don't want you. I love you, but I can't leave him. I need you, but I can't give up my promiscuity." Even the loner who fantasizes about sexy women while he masturbates is engaged in an unreal relationship while making love to himself. The woman who says she never looks at another man and is in fact absolutely faithful to her husband may fantasize about falling in love. Wherever we find love addiction we will find this threesome—me, you, and the fantasy lover.

It's no coincidence that this love triangle re-creates the situation of childhood. Nearly all of us have fantasized about being the lover to our opposite-sex parent, while at the same time needing to identify with our same-sex parent. Those who have a preference for same-sex partners have certain unique issues to deal with, yet much of what we know about love addiction applies equally to heterosexual and homosexual relationships.

For now, it will help us to understand the approach-avoidance dance if we recall a number of key points discussed in chapter 1. We search desperately for someone who will love and accept us, a person we can feel safe with, but deep down inside we don't believe anyone can be trusted. The result of this belief is that when we are alone we want more than anything else to find a person we can connect with. Once we have made the connection, we do everything we can to get close. When we fall in love, we fall hard. But the closer we get the more vulnerable we become. The hidden fear and distrust, usually buried beyond our conscious awareness, take over and we begin to withdraw.

Fantasy lovers serve the purpose of protecting us from getting too close to this real lover. I heard a radio commercial recently that featured a humanoid computer saying "Never trust a man with skin." That's how we feel when we get too close. People with "skin" are unpredictable and potentially threatening. Having had early family experiences with people we could not trust, we learned that it was safer to "love" a fantasy.

But we aren't comfortable being mated to a fantasy. We miss the "skin" and want to return to a real-life partner. We are caught. Love addicts can't give up the fantasy lover because they are sure they will die if they do, and they can't give up looking for genuine love because to give that up will kill them. The result is that we are forced to deaden ourselves. As we feel more wooden inside, we seek ever increasing emotional intrigue in order to feel alive.

As one man described this dilemma: "I didn't have the courage to leave my wife, and I didn't have the guts to cut off the affair and deal with my marriage honestly. My feelings became more and more deadened as my life became more compartmentalized. The only way I knew I was alive was the intense feelings of excitement I got from trying to juggle the various aspects of my romantic life."

Addiction and the Family

Traditionally we have viewed addiction as resulting from an interaction between a person and a chemical substance. We spent a great deal of time focusing on the nature of the chemical itself to help us understand the nature of addiction.

A major breakthrough in our understanding of addiction came when we began to see that the entire family was involved.[1] We came to see that the various addictions weren't just the result of

97

the interaction between an individual and a chemical, but resulted also from an interaction with individuals in the family. We learned that spouses could actually increase the power of the addiction through their "enabling" or "blaming" behavior.

This led us to question the role of the family of origin as well as the contemporary family. We learned that having one or more blood relatives who were alcoholic or chemically dependent increased the risk of becoming addicted ourselves.

This emphasis on family role has helped us understand that being in an intimate relationship with an addict—being a co-addict—is just as much an addiction as being hooked oneself. Focusing the knowledge gained in the area of chemical addiction on the areas of sex and love addiction, we now better understand women who continually fall in love with men who are unavailable or abusive. We now know how women are trained to love too much and we can now teach them how to love wisely and well.

With our emphasis on women, however, we have neglected the other side of the coin—men who lust too much. For every woman who loves too much there is a man who lusts too much. And for every woman who finds herself hooked on an endless search for romantic intrigue, there is a man who becomes so dependent on a woman that he sacrifices everything to keep her close. In order to get a more complete understanding of human relationships we must turn our attention to the male side of the picture, which has been so long neglected.

Men, Women, and Romance

Traditionally women are conditioned to have a primary need for *connection*. Their deepest fear is of *abandonment* or *loss*. In the romantic arena, they are taught to withhold sex and trade it for a secure home. In the process they learn to deny their enjoyment of sex and become "mini-masochists," as Dr. Warren Farrell describes them.

Men, on the other hand, are conditioned to need *space*. Their deepest fear is being *smothered* or *bound*. Men are taught to withhold their commitment and trade it for the sexual favors that women withhold. In the process they learn to overemphasize sex, to become hypersexual. As Dr. Farrell so aptly points out, men are conditioned to become "mini-rapists."[2] They become preoccupied with the very thing women withhold, believing that they can only receive sex if they force a woman to give it to them. The force may be subtle or overt, but it is a part of male conditioning.

Roy Schenk describes the female perspective on making love as a "sexual rainforest" in which sex is always dripping down on them.[3] They can never get away from it and feel oppressed by it. Women who say they can't ever have a quiet meal alone in a restaurant without men leering at them experience the sexual rainforest.

Men, on the other hand, says Schenk, have the experience of a sexual desert. They are always searching for sex and constantly feel in danger of dying for lack of sexual nourishment. They feel oppressed by the power women have to withhold something so vital to life. Men who say they could eat in a restaurant alone for twenty years without having a woman so much as smile at them experience the sexual desert.

As men and women have shed their traditional sex roles, they have become more liberated. But many have simply traded one set of constraints for another. Many men now deny their sexuality and become masochists and many women have developed the hypersexuality and aggressiveness of the rapist. (We will discuss more about the changing roles of men and women later in this chapter.) Couples often experience this ebb and flow as an "approach-avoidance dance." One of the painful ironies of modern life seems to be that we are rarely in tune with each other. He wants space when she wants to be close. Just when he wants to connect, she wants to explore the world.

Much has been written in recent years about the woman's side of the dance.[4] But little attention has been paid to the corresponding male steps. It is to this that we now turn. To understand the dance and be able to change it, we need to understand the male side of the equation.

Male Conditioning

We pointed out earlier that one of the reasons we haven't recognized love addiction before is that it is so much a part of our culture it has become invisible. I would go a step further now and say that we have neglected love addiction because we have not recognized the ways in which male conditioning leads to it. Although female conditioning can also lead to addiction, it has gotten more attention than male conditioning.[5]

Let's think about those factors that are at the core of all addiction and how they also are at the core of male conditioning. Although addicts may feel effective in doing in the world (professional life), they feel rotten inside at the level of their being (emotional life).[6] As we look at the ways men are conditioned in our society, we get a better understanding of the ways couples relate and the roots of love addiction.

As little boys we learned that to be male was to be mean, violent, warlike. And whatever we were, little girls were the opposite. "Little girls are made of sugar and spice and everything nice." It's no wonder that we grow up needing them and hating them at the same time.

Men are taught that they are bad inside, that the goodness they seek is in the opposite sex, hence something that can't be developed but must be acquired. They come to believe that they must have a woman in order to have those qualities they lack.

In order to "get a woman" who will love us, we try to emphasize the "manly" qualities that we do have. In the process of being supermasculine, we exclude any qualities that seem "feminine."

We develop the same "disease" as the woman we discussed earlier who got more and more protective of the one spring as she got ill from lack of nutrients in the other. That is the nature of addiction. We come to neglect the very things we need in order to grow and can't seem to get enough of the things that are harming us.

Men develop a whole series of qualities that they must be in order to be "good" men—and hence attract a "good" woman— and another set of qualities that they must not be unless they want to be seen as less than men, i.e., as women or homosexuals.[7]

100

Men must be: tall, physically strong, economically powerful, courageous, cool, stoic, protective of women and children, good breadwinners, logical, active, aggressive, hairy, outspoken, rugged, tough. I remember a cartoon of a woman and man sitting across from each other at a dinner table. He looks like a "real man." He sits there with a fork embedded in his nose, obviously having been stabbed by the woman. The caption reads: "That's what I like about you, Louie, you're tough." Men learn to suppress pain, to fight other men, but to let women abuse them and suffer in silence.

There is a parallel list of qualities that men are taught they cannot be.

Men must not be: short, loving, nurturing, tender, feeling, domestic, beautiful, apologetic, curvy, thin, passive, receptive, nice, sweet, hairless, quiet, giving, soft.

It isn't surprising that men often feel themselves to be half a person. That's a very painful state of being, like growing up without arms or legs. The core of addiction is the search for the parts of ourselves that we feel are lacking and trying to stop the pain we feel from being mutilated.

From Abused Boys to Violent Men

Several years ago I worked at a shelter for battered women. It was heartbreaking to see women with small children come into the shelter who had been beaten by their husbands or lovers. My job was to work with the men. At first it was difficult to feel much sympathy toward the men, much less care for them. They didn't talk much, though they seemed to carry a great deal of pain. I remember my shock when one of the men finally opened himself up and told about his own childhood.

"My dad was a policeman and I loved him with blind devotion." Robert was a big man, his hands callused from construction work. He had been referred to me after having been arrested for beating his wife and whipping his three-year-old son with a belt on numerous occasions. We had been meeting for many months, but Robert had never been willing to talk about his past except to say it was "okay."

101

Robert continued: "I didn't see my father a lot as a child but I used to run to him and throw my arms around his neck when he'd come in the door. I remember a game we played when I was maybe two or three years old. I would climb up on a chair and yell Catch Me! as I'd jump into his arms squealing with delight.

"I remember the day it happened, clear as if it was yesterday," Robert said. His expression didn't change. Only something deep in his eyes revealed his feelings. "I yelled out 'Daddy, Daddy!' as I jumped off the kitchen chair and flew through the air with my arms outstretched. But just as I reached out to him, he turned away and I hit my head on the table as I fell to the floor. I don't remember much after that except Dad yelling at me to be quiet as we drove to the hospital. Days later . . ." Robert's gaze was steady as he remembered his father's words. I couldn't hold back the tears that ran down my own cheeks when he continued: "Dad took me on his lap and said 'Baby boy, you have to learn—you can't trust anyone in this life, not even your own father.' "

Robert breathed a sigh. "I've never really remembered that scene until recently. I just know that I never again reached out for him. Something died in me that day, or got buried, I don't know." Robert paused for a long time. "There were other lessons along the way to 'make me tough.' I never resented them at the time. I just thought that's what it was like to be a boy and grow up to be a man. But I missed jumping into the arms of my dad."

It took Robert a long while to express his rage and the hurt and fear that went with it. It took him a long time to express the guilt he felt at just being and finally to rediscover the understanding and love of his father that had been buried so long ago. For his whole life he had hated his father, swore he would never be like him. Now he found that he was repeating many of the same violent behaviors. Being able to forgive his father and actually to recognize that his father loved him began to free Robert to love himself and his family.

As I heard from more and more men like Robert who had done horrible things to women and children, I came to see that there was another side to them. My sympathy for the victims of violence

102

and abuse began to extend to the victimizers as well. Every man I worked with at the shelter was himself a victim of abuse when he was a child. Inside every cold, violent Robert was a little boy calling out "Daddy, Daddy, catch me, Daddy!" as he saw the floor instead of his father coming up to meet him.

We can only speculate on what it must have been like for Robert's father to watch his son screaming, his face bloody, as he taught the lessons he thought his son needed to learn. What was *his* father like, we wonder, and where will the cycle of violence end? The traditional male conditioning to be "tough" is surely to blame.

It is also, I believe, to blame for aspects of the AIDS epidemic. As I've indicated before, like many things that are so common, addictive love goes unnoticed often. Like the air around us, as long as we breathe easily, we aren't even aware of its presence. In the case of AIDS, we have neglected to pay enough attention to the fact that many homosexuals and IV drug addicts are also sexual addicts. Until we begin to ask how it is that men have become so compulsive about sex and romance, we will be missing an important part of the puzzle in understanding AIDS. Sexual addiction and the epidemic spread of AIDS are intimately related, yet few seem to be aware of this important psychological connection.

Parenting

What are the implications of the fact that in Western cultures boys have so little contact with their fathers as compared with their mothers as they grow up? The long dependency of the human infant is a biological fact. Yet it is a cultural fact that a woman, usually the biological mother, is the primary caregiver in infancy. Experts feel this fact is crucial for adult development.[8]

In our culture, until very recently, men were generally barred from the delivery room and it was the mother who was with her infant from the very first hours of birth. No fact of our early life has greater consequences for how boys and girls develop into men and women, how they form love relationships, and how sexual addictions develop.

103

Mothering is an all-embracing word. To be mothered is to be nurtured in the most elemental sense—to be cared for in all the ways we might wish or need, from the physical to the psychological and spiritual. But what does fathering mean?[9] The fact that it is so nebulous says a lot about the vague feelings we have toward our fathers, husbands, and men in general. The fact that women provide for our most intimate needs for survival, security, love, and affection says a great deal about the differences between men and women and the ways in which men develop love addictions.

From early on it is the mother who is the primary caregiver—the person who feeds us, shelters us, protects us, comforts us, holds us in her arms to allay our fears. It is she with whom we make our first attachment, she with whom we form the closest of human bonds before we even know where "we" leave off and "others" begin.

For each of us, then, whether a girl or a boy, it is a woman who holds this primary position in our inner life—a woman who is the object of our most profound attachment, a woman who becomes our first love object. Yet we all must separate to become fully human, we must move beyond mother to become our own unique selves. Thus separation and unity—being attracted to others and being attached to one person, seeking and merging—are themes that are central our whole lives.

For every child each separation feels like an abandonment and each abandonment feels like a threat to life itself. Those of us who grew up in homes that were chaotic developed more deep-seated fears for our very lives than did other children.

When we experience the first stirrings of adult intimacy we experience again those early struggles around separation and unity—the conflict between wanting to merge with another human being and the desire for an independent, autonomous self.

When we fall in love, we not only experience the excitement as an adult but rekindle the esctasy of infancy. We feel in our bones the bliss of being united again with our mother, safe and secure in her arms. But unconsciously we also feel the agony of abandonment. We remember life as an endless series of separations. We remember every love that was lost and all the losses yet to come, each one experienced as a threat to survival itself.

104

Men and Love

For little boys, fears about losing mother have special implications, since there is a difference between the love lives of men and those of women. Most men will fall in love with a person of the same sex as their mothers, while most women will fall in love with a person of the opposite sex. Thus for men, the early experience of their first love object is more closely re-created as they connect again in adulthood with a woman. It's therefore easier for men to become hooked, and their love feelings are more ambivalent.

For a boy to establish his male identity he must renounce his early connection with the woman (his mother). He must cut off the first person to be internalized into his inner psychic world and seek instead an attachment and identification with his father.

Think what it is like for the baby boy to realize: "I am different from mother." That is the first great setback. He must renounce his first true love. The second is that when he reaches out for this other person, this father, who he should aspire to grow up to emulate, who he can identify with, he often finds this person is missing. (The fact that fathers are absent for girls as well has its own implications for the development of female love addiction, about which more will be said later.)

The aggressiveness that is supposed to be inherent in men can be better explained as a reaction to this early experience of having to relinquish the first person we had ever loved in favor of a father who is often absent.[10] The anger toward women can be seen as a response to that early loss and the sense of betrayal that went with it. A man feels that it was a woman who abandoned him to the shadowy and alien world of men. How then could she—or any woman—ever be wholly trusted again? Add to that the numerous ways in which little boys are treated roughly and the countless ways in which aggression between and toward males is condoned in the society, and we begin to have a more complete understanding of men's anger toward women.

If the world of men, as represented by our fathers, is absent, we feel a hole inside. If men are seen as dangerous or threatening, this also breeds fear in little boys. Either way, men remember their earliest connection to their mothers as a "paradise lost." They long for the feeling of security that they felt in the mythical mists of early infancy. Fathers, and men in general, are too distant to offer any hope of getting love and nurturing. The addictive patterns are set in motion. We feel we must have women in order to survive, but we don't trust them, and we carry a deeply felt rage at being abandoned and betrayed.

The rage little boys develop from feeling abandoned is fostered as they grow up and accept more of the male role. We are told that we derive value in the world only from our "actions," from what we "do." A girl need only "be" in order to feel a sense of identity, a boy must always "produce." We become breadwinners and feel we must carry the burden not just for ourselves but for our families as well.

We distrust other men, since they are seen as our competitors for the success we seek. This success should allow us to have the kind of woman that success can attract. We must kill off our ability to love and care for other men since we can't let ourselves get too close to our rivals.

Finally, we learn that little boys will grow up to be soldiers and will be asked to kill others and be willing to die in the name of "manhood." Our greatest fear is to be labeled a coward, afraid to die in support of manly ideals. From playing with toy guns as cowboys and Indians to the battlefields of Vietnam, we learn that we must kill or be killed.

Most women can't conceive of what this is like for men, just as most men have great difficulty understanding what it would be like to carry a baby inside or feel so merged with "mother" that you can't separate and develop your own identity. If you are a woman reading this book, ask yourself what would have to be done to you for you to be willing to kill other women and die yourself, in the name of your womanhood? I asked this question at a conference on domestic violence attended by both men and women. One woman finally replied with tears running down her cheeks, "I would have to kill off my feelings. I would have to be brutalized so badly that I had lost all human emotions." Many women understood male violence in a new way after this, and their understanding deepened

106

after a number of male batterers told about their own abusive childhoods.

Understanding male conditioning also helps us get a clearer picture of the contempt men often feel for women and the ways men try to control them. Both these feelings—the need to control and the contempt—are at the center of men's love addiction. For the boy, his fear is so great that he can live with it only by rigidly controlling the woman and making her powerless. He can use her for his pleasure because she is "weak" and "deserves" to be hurt and humiliated. In this way he can express his rage and anger at having to sever his connection to mother while simultaneously protecting himself from the fear of "big mother" attacking him. This is why in pornography the women always come to enjoy being abused. They ask to be hurt. Only in this kind of fantasy can the man protect himself against abusing a woman who might really be strong enough to retaliate.

For the girl, the situation is different. For her, the first lover is female, just like her. It is easier for her to identify with mother and to see that eventually she can be like her when she grows up. Since she need not displace the internalized representation of the beloved mother, there's no need to build defenses against feeling and attachment, no need therefore for the kind of rigid boundaries a man develops as a means of protecting and maintaining those defenses. The great difficulty women have is in developing a separate identity, since their boundaries are so much more permeable than those of men. They often fall into the trap of "giving themselves away" in order to get love.

The Core of Romantic Addiction

When women develop love addictions, they usually get hooked on the romance, the feeling of losing themselves in another person. One woman expressed it this way: "One smile and I'm entranced. A touch melts my insides. And when he kisses me, I'm lost. I fall hopelessly in love."

Men in love develop the opposite problem. Out of fear they try to control and dominate. They want to retain their feeling of separateness at all costs and often isolate their sexual and emotional feelings from each other. One man recalled a typical physical encounter: "Once she said yes to my advances I wanted to conquer her. My lust turned to rage and I wanted to make her pay for all the pretty young things who had rejected me when I needed them the most."

So, to recapitulate, from the very beginning men develop a pattern of relating to women in which the men are dependent on women for their most basic needs—safety and security. Since they frequently don't have the support of the father, they fail to develop a strong sense of themselves. Hence they need women but don't have the inner identity that allows them to feel like a whole person deserving of love. They develop a feeling of "entitlement" in order to ensure that the woman will be there for them. Women learn the complementary role. They learn to "merge" with their loved one, to gain their identity by giving of themselves.

This core of the addictive process is then reinforced as little boys and little girls grow up to be men and women. We each are looking for the "other" part of us so that we can feel complete. Each is taught that we have to give up some part of ourselves in order to get that other part. Men often give up the soft, yielding qualities of the feminine while women give up the assertive, strong masculine qualities. We bond with a lover in order to feel the familiar feeling of "coming home."

Ironically, however, we can only feel whole and complete if the other person never deviates from their role, but this means acting unreal, not human. Any deviation is felt as a threat to our very survival. The fear at the core of our being never disappears and we develop our love obsessions in an attempt to quiet the feelings and fill the void. We are rarely aware of this internal struggle. Usually we blame our partner when the feelings get really bad. Listen as one of my client couples plays out a typical scene from the approach-avoidance dance.

WIFE: "You revolt me. All you ever think about is sex. I feel like a piece of meat when I'm around you. What's the use? If you're not lusting after me, you're either reading one of your porno magazines or undressing the waitress or any other woman you can get your eyes on. Can't you treat women like people?"

HUSBAND: "Jesus Christ! What do you expect? Every time I show my interest in you, you're too busy or you have a headache or you just look at me with that look that would kill. Do you know what it's like making love with someone who lets you know they're revolted by you? [Turning to me:] Sometimes I get so goddamned mad, I feel like busting someone in the face."

WIFE: "That's another thing. I'm afraid of you. I'm never sure what you might do to me or the kids. I want some hugs and kisses. I want some tenderness from you. But as soon as you touch me, the damn thing gets hard and I know all you're thinking about is having sex."

HUSBAND: "What do you expect me to feel? [With a lowered voice that sounds more hurt than angry.] I love you. You're my wife. I want us to be happy like we were. Of course I get excited when we're close. We haven't had sex in three weeks. You say all I can think about is sex. For me I feel like a man dying of thirst in the desert. Don't you understand that a man who has been for days without water has water on his mind all the time?"

WIFE: "I don't understand how you can want to make love when there's so much distance between us. I need to feel close before I want to make love . . ."

HUSBAND: [Interrupting excitedly] "I want to make love so we *can* feel close again!"

This is a dance that goes on every day in thousands of homes throughout the world. Rarely do people bring the conflict to a third party. Sex is too private, most of us think. We would rather suffer in our private hells or start an affair than do the hard work to clear things up together.

The Erotic/Emotional Split

A number of researchers and clinicians theorize that for a boy it is the emotional component of the attachment to the mother that comes under attack as he seeks to repress his identification with her.[11] The feeling of "I can't be like mother, because I'm a boy and she's a girl" forces boys to cut off their emotional attachment so that they can identify with their fathers. The erotic, or sexualized, aspect of the motherly attachment is left undisturbed (in heterosexual men).

For girls, the opposite is true. For her, it's the erotic, sexual component of the attachment to a woman that must be denied and shifted later to a man; the larger emotional involvement and the identification remain intact (in heterosexual women).

For men, the erotic aspect of any relationship remains forever the most compelling, while for women, the emotional component will always be primary. For women, the sexual aspect retains little independent status in her inner life.

A man may lust after *women,* but a woman lusts after only one particular man. Women depend on the emotional attachment to open up their sexual feelings, while men rely on the sexual link to spark the emotional bond. This split between the erotic and the emotional has implications for both men and women and for our understanding of romantic and sexual addictions.

Let's follow the implications for men as we listen to one man trying to make sense out of his love addiction: "I have a reputation for being a "woman's man," Gregory said. He looked the part. He was tall and muscular from the hours he spent working on various construction jobs. "But to be honest with you, sex can also be a problem for me. If I don't keep a lid on it, so much begins to happen that I get scared. I have real difficulty letting myself go with a woman I really love. So much gets stirred up in me, I kinda put a damper on things.

"I'm a little ashamed to say it, but I can do a whole lot better romantically when I'm with a woman I don't feel too close to. Don't get me wrong, I don't mean going to prostitutes. I just mean I feel more comfortable in some ways with a woman I don't really feel in love with. When I'm with Karen, the girl that I love, I feel anxious most of the time when we're making love.

"With Karen, sometimes I feel like I want to be with her and never let go and sometimes I get scared, like I'm going to lose my very existence.

"I can't quite put my finger on it. The closest I can get is to say it feels like something dark and secret." Gregory paused and I could almost see his heart pounding. "Let's see. It's something like this. If I let it all happen—I mean if I really let myself go, give up control, you know, let all those feelings come out—I don't know where it would all end. It's like a person could get lost in them. I get a picture in my mind of going into a dark cave with an endless number of passageways. Once inside, I immediately get lost and I know I'll never get out alive."

Gregory stops and laughs. "This sounds too much like some kind of Freudian shit. I've heard people say sex is like going back to the womb. I don't know about that. I do feel, though, that when I'm with a woman I love, sex has a double edge to it. I love it and want it, but I also feel like I could get lost in it. Sometimes I feel like a little kid who doesn't want to grow up. It scares the hell out of me. What would I do if I liked it so much I never wanted to go out in the world again?"

We become afraid of our own dependency, concerned that if we ever let our feelings out with someone we loved, they would overwhelm and trap us. Love addiction becomes a very attractive way of dealing with our feelings. We place our energy in people and situations that don't arouse our emotions. Men often feel torn between their desire for a "whore" and for a "madonna." Sometimes this split feeds our addiction by allowing us to love our wife at home while lusting after other women.

Women Addicts/Male Co-addicts

Traditionally, it has been men who have acted out this conflict sexually. Thus, the majority of sexually addictive relationships involve a male addict and a female co-addict. As women have become more liberated in the last ten years, however, they have sought the privileges once enjoyed by men. Many have sought greater degrees of romantic and sexual freedom. Often neglected in our focus on

111

sexual liberation has been the increase in the number of women who have developed love addictions. At recent recovery meetings I have attended, the groups were about equally divided between males and females.

The increase in female love addiction is borne out both through anecdote and research. Dear Abby reports that ten years ago 90 percent of those having extramarital affairs were men and 10 percent were women. Now she reports the figures are about 50–50.

A researcher corroborates the increased degree to which women are beginning to objectify men. They are beginning to separate sex from love in the same destructive ways that men have done traditionally. The study says that "Women in their oral histories revealed the 'objectification' of men, not only as potential 'marriage object' but as a 'sexual object.' " The women also reported that they think the emphasis on looks is one of the biggest mistakes women make. The Greek Adonis often turns out to be the devil in disguise, some women say."[12]

Role reversals have begun to affect men as well. Some have shed the old "macho" role and have learned to be more caring and nurturing. But many men have now become overly giving and have taken on many of the characteristics of the traditional female co-addict—fearful of being abandoned, needy, dependent, hooked on attachment.

Bob and Cindy are typical of many New Age couples I have seen lately. Bob is a stockbroker and Cindy owns her own small clothing store. They have been married for ten years. Both were married once before; Cindy's fifteen-year-old daughter, Sarah, from her previous marriage, lives with the couple. They've decided not to have other children. Cindy's career has taken off over the past few years, while Bob's has remained static.

Bob first came to see me complaining of feeling extremely jealous of Cindy and wanting help sorting out his feelings. On first meeting, he was soft-spoken and gentle in manner. He had a well-trimmed mustache and seemed genuinely concerned about his feelings toward his wife. "I don't know what's the matter with me lately," he began. "I've begun to have these terrible feelings of jealousy whenever Cindy and I go out together. I imagine that she's looking at other men all the time. When we're apart I'm always wondering who she might be with or what she's doing. I never used to be like this."

As he talked about their relationship, it seems that it had changed a good deal in the twelve years since they first met. At that time she was quite content to stay home with Sarah and he was happy to be the breadwinner. Cindy was loving and attentive and was happy to take care of Bob, Sarah, and the house. "She was always a party girl," Bob said. "We met at a New Year's Eve bash. She was dancing with all the guys, sitting on everyone's lap. She was the life of the party. I'm not sure what attracted her to me. Maybe because I didn't seem to chase after her like the other guys did. I just sat quietly and watched. At first I was really indifferent to her and that seemed to stimulate her interest. Our romance was a whirlwind. I never met anyone with so much excitement and energy. After spending the weekend together, I needed three days to recuperate.

"After we were married she seemed to settle down to staying with Sarah. I was away a fair amount and loved to come home to her waiting arms. Her only complaint was that she didn't see me enough and we didn't have enough time together. By then, I had lost interest in work. It had become pretty easy and routine. We made good money, so I thought I'd cut back my hours. I found I really liked being home. I got very involved with Sarah's school and I would go to all the PTA meetings and school events.

"It was strange. The more involved I got at home, the more restless Cindy became. I thought she'd be overjoyed to have more time to be together. But she seemed to get bored with our activities. Finally, she decided to open up a dress shop. As soon as she got started she brightened up. At first I was glad she had something that really occupied her time. But lately she doesn't have time for us and she's often home late."

Bob seemed quite sad. His shoulders slumped slightly as he continued. "I don't mind cooking and doing more cleaning around the house. In fact, I enjoy making food for us. But I miss Cindy."

After a number of sessions with Bob, Cindy asked to see me. It was obvious that she knew about clothes. She was dressed in a

113

beautiful long skirt with matching blouse and scarf. She looked like a fashion model, but with the excitement and energy of a college cheerleader.

"I love Bob a lot," she began, "and I really don't want to hurt him, but there's a lot about me he doesn't know. When Bob and I met, I had been recently divorced, and I really wasn't ready to settle down." She paused and looked down at her hands. "In fact, I've never really been able to settle down, even during my first marriage. I've always considered myself a 'liberated woman.' If it was okay for men to mess around, it seemed like it should be okay for women too. When I was single, I would see a lot of different men. I loved the excitement of a new romance. But after a while it started to get me down. I knew I had to do something when I woke up with a man and couldn't even remember his name. And besides, Sarah needed a more stable home life. When I met Bob, I thought it would help me settle down. He was so quiet and stable. Unlike a lot of the men I met, he didn't seem to mind that I had a small child and he even seemed to like playing with Sarah.

"For a while things were great. I loved staying home with Sarah and I thought I had gotten 'men' out of my system. Bob was so loving and caring I felt like a queen. But something seemed to happen." Tears came to her eyes. "I started to get bored. Bob felt more like a brother than a lover. Jesus, he's like a puppy dog most of the time. He's loyal and good and caring." She paused. "And so goddamned dull I could scream!

"I began going out to lunch with one of the reps who sells to the store. We'd have a few drinks and he would joke about getting me in the back room and making love to me until I couldn't walk without limping. He was vulgar and I didn't like the way he talked to me, but it was strangely arousing.

"Well, one thing led to another and we had a brief fling. I don't want to endanger the relationship with Bob. I'd like him to get mad or confront me about my lack of interest, or *something*. He's so damn nice, I can't stand it!" Cindy took a deep breath and continued. "I guess it's up to me. I really want to stop thinking about this guy and put more time into my relationship with Bob, but I can't get him out of my mind. Does that sound terrible?"

114

The New Man and the New Woman

This phenomenon of "the passive man and the wild woman" is becoming increasingly common.[13] As women become more involved in the world of business and have access to attractive men, they too are experiencing the pressures that men once felt. Although the fear of AIDS is currently causing both men and women to be much more restrictive in their expression of physical intimacy, it hasn't lessened their interest in romance. But for many like Cindy, the freedom to pursue romance with anyone who is attractive and available quickly becomes an addiction. Family and personal lives are threatened. And the payoff—romantic excitement and intrigue—becomes less and less attractive as the compulsion increases, which always happens in addictive behavior.

As women get caught in the same traps of addictive love that have long been so common to men, so too are men becoming hooked by the same co-addictive behavior that women have been so susceptible to in the past. As men have been able to let go of the old stereotypes of masculinity, they have become more comfortable with the soft, gentle sides of their personalities, often rejecting traditional views of male/female relationships in which women are seen as objects to be used for men's pleasure.

In seeking to understand the women we were with, to feel their pain, and to comfort and care for them, we accepted that their needs were as important as our own. We wanted them to "find themselves." However, there was something missing. We were able to help the woman in our life find what she needed but we found it difficult to know what we wanted ourselves.

I remember being involved with a "liberated woman" who was quite open about telling me exactly what she liked and what she didn't like about our lovemaking. She would tell me she wanted it softer or harder, that she wanted me to touch her here or there, that she liked my tongue on this spot, but not on that one. I was glad to be with a woman who knew what she wanted and wasn't afraid to tell me and show me how to make her happy. But when she asked me what I liked about sex, I became confused.

I realized that beyond the excitement of pornographic sex, I

115

didn't have any idea what my body liked. I knew it turned me on to see her turned on, to feel that I could make her writhe with passion, but when I tried to tune into my own body to see what I liked and didn't like, I felt strangely mute.

This ability to give pleasure but not to feel pleasure, to be receptive but not active, to make others happy but not be happy ourselves is happening to more and more men. From the time of Vietnam, many of us put away the role of the macho warrior in favor of a gentle warrior who brings peace rather than death to the world. This is good. We have been more receptive to Mother Earth and more caring about the environment. We are in the delivery rooms when our children are born and more available to them as they are growing.

However, we have also lost something important in the process. In trying to be more human and more caring toward women, we have allowed women to define for us what it means to be a man.

Many of us who had absent or abusive fathers have a very shaky sense of our own masculinity. As women become more liberated and define more clearly the kind of person they want to be, they also define the kind of man they want to be with.

Mutual Romantic Addictions

In our desire to find the life and excitement we somehow lost, and afraid to look for it from other men who we have come to see as aggressive and hostile, we find ourselves increasingly attracted to strong women. But we can't get "male" strength from a female. Rather than making us feel stronger and more attractive, strong women actually make us feel weaker and more passive. The woman who was initially attracted to our gentleness and kindness comes to hate and despise us. Having sold out our own sense of who we are, imperfect though it may be, for the "ideal" we think the woman wants, we find ourselves in danger of losing the woman for whom we have changed. We feel abandoned and deceived, but don't know where to turn. Often we cling more and more tightly to a woman, we get hooked on her, and we get hooked on the pain we feel.

Bob and Cindy found as they began to work on their relationship that the first step for each was to be able to acknowledge their respective addictions. Cindy found she needed to put an end to her affairs in order to confront her fears about getting truly close to Bob. He had to develop enough outside supports in his life so that he could risk the possibility of losing her while he regained confidence in himself.

Most of us fall into the approach-avoidance dance without noticing it. We become enmeshed in addictive relationships without being conscious of the process. As you reflect on your life and consider what you've learned about love addiction from your reading up to this point, you will have a better basis for moving ahead.

The first step in getting anywhere is being able to see where we are. You may want to go directly to Part III—Getting Free—for help in overcoming your addiction. Or you may wish to continue on to Part II to get a further understanding of how people become love addicts.

How People Get Hooked

5. YOU ARE MY SECURITY BLANKET

Underlying Causes of Addiction

If you are addicted to love or care about someone who is, you are probably less concerned about how a person gets that way than you are about how to get free. Yet understanding the addictive process can be very helpful in finding a way out of it. In the field of addictions there is a great deal of disagreement about the underlying causes.

Some say that addictions are physiological problems and that we inherit a genetic susceptibility toward them. Others believe that addictions are caused by faulty interpersonal relationships that develop within the family as we grow up. Some believe the causes lie in our psychological make-up and our beliefs about ourselves, while others feel strongly that they are caused by the stresses generated by society. Many are convinced that our peer group contributes to our chances of becoming addicted.

My experience is that addictions are caused by multiple factors. To help a specific individual we must attend to genetic, family, psychological, interpersonal, and social factors. When someone comes into my office seeking help, I assume that all factors are present to some degree in the person's life. In my initial interviews and throughout the treatment process, I ask myself how much each factor contributes to their present problem and how this knowledge can be used to aid in recovery.

In this section I would like to explore a number of factors I have found crucial in understanding how people get hooked, but that are often neglected by those working in the field of addictions. I would like to focus first on the issue of child abuse and the threat to security I have found so prevalent in working with people who have love addictions.

Growing Up Afraid and Unprotected

The experience of abuse that clients have reported to me runs the gamut from the seemingly trivial to the most blatant. The common factor I've found in the addicts I've treated is that they grew up feeling fearful and unsafe.

Carol, the woman recovering from alcoholism whom we met in chapter 1, took two years before she was able to talk to me about her love life and the anger she was feeling toward her husband. It took another six months before she was able to tie in her anger toward her husband to childhood experiences that seriously undermined her feeling of safety and security.

Like most clients who are dealing with addictions, Carol needed to focus on present issues during the first two years of treatment. Only later was it appropriate to explore the past. When our lives begin to get out of control and the house of cards we've so carefully built begins to tumble, our attention is on the present moment. How can I hold things together? What can I do to survive? This is the time when we need immediate support that will provide the safety and security to deal with the present crisis and lay the foundation for exploring the life patterns that have led to this particular point in our lives. Once her life had become stabilized, Carol began to explore the past experiences that contributed to her present dilemma.

For most of us, our families are almost invisible. They are so integrally a part of our lives that we are often blind to the influence

122

of parents, grandparents, siblings, and other important family members. Until we begin to hear other people's stories and compare them to our own our family life just "is." That's one of the reasons it's so important for people in recovery to be in some kind of support group.

When I first ask someone what it was like growing up in their family, they often get a kind of blank stare. "I don't know, okay, I guess."

We only recognize something as "hot" by contrasting it with something that is "cold." If we have no conception of "warm weather," living in Minnesota in the winter feels fine. It's what we know. Until we are old enough to compare our own family situation to that of others, growing up in an abusive family feels normal.

A very large proportion of people with love addictions have experienced some form of abuse as children. For many the experiences were so traumatic that they literally can't remember that period of their life. Often there is a feeling that "something happened but I can't quite get a picture of it." It is important to bring these memories to the surface so that the past can be laid to rest. However, the process must be done with care and support and only at the client's own pace.

When Carol began to remember her early life she began to share, little by little, experiences that showed the degree of rigidity, fear, and abuse that were present. Her mother was an alcoholic who went on and off the wagon and her father was a businessman who wanted more than anything else in the world to make money. At first she said she couldn't remember anything in her life before the age of nine.

"It's a total blank," she said. "I just know I wasn't happy and wanted to get out as quickly as possible." Her most vivid memory was of running away from home following her high school graduation and getting a job in another town. "I felt free for the first time in my life," she said, smiling one of her rare smiles. "But then my father came and took me back home."

I was surprised. "You mean he physically forced you to return home?" I asked. "No, he didn't actually force me." She was beginning to get angry now. Her words were clipped and short. "But

123

I felt I had to go with him." She seemed momentarily confused. "I don't know how to say it, I just felt he had power over me."

It took many months of therapy to uncover the power her father had over her. During that time I encouraged Carol to continue her active involvement in AA. I talked often with her sponsor and made every effort to ensure that she continued to develop a firm foundation of sobriety while we explored the roots of her love addiction. I felt sure that she would never be able to achieve real happiness until she came to peace with her past. I also knew it would be useless to clean up her past and confront her love addiction if she returned to alcohol.

Carol was ambivalent about "finding out" about the relationship between herself and her father. At times she would say, "I've got to know. It's a shadow that hangs over me and is ruining my life." At other times, she would say, "I don't want to know. Can't we just move on and forget this part?" I always let her move at her own speed, but told her honestly that I felt she needed to face the hidden fear she was carrying.

Over time, Carol began to remember vague feelings of being touched inappropriately by her father when she was a child. When we would talk about it, there was a feeling of disbelief. "I can't believe my father would have done something like that," she said with her usual irritation. "I mean, he wasn't a great father but he just couldn't . . ."

We are just now beginning to accept the reality of child abuse. For most, it is almost inconceivable that it could have happened to us or someone we love. Yet child abuse and molestation are much more common than we ever believed. Often the most hurtful kind of abuse happens when a child is very young and so isn't able to remember the specifics of what happened. They grow up with a vague sense of dread that becomes more pronounced when they become intimate as adults.

As Carol began to accept the fact that "something" had happened even though she was not yet able to remember what it was, she began to be able to understand her present fear and anger toward men. She could also understand the ways she blamed herself for these vague feelings of having done something wrong.

124

Overcoming Shame and Guilt

For love addicts, even more than for alcoholics and drug addicts, shame and guilt have become part of us. Our greatest fear is that by acknowledging our behavior, even to ourselves, we will be consumed by the knowledge of what we have done.

At this stage of recovery it is essential that you be able to see, if only for an instant, that you are *not* to blame for what happened to you. As children, totally dependent on our parents for our survival, we needed to see them as blameless. If there was a conflict, we would naturally see ourselves at fault. To have done otherwise would have put our very existence in jeopardy. If we were to blame, we could try harder to be good. If our parents were to blame, there would be no hope.

As adults we must now learn to stop blaming ourselves and expose our lives to the light. We have spent many years hiding our "horrible" selves so that no one would see us. Now we must take the first tentative steps to reveal our fears, little by little, to another human being who will not judge us or reject us.

As I could accept Carol fully in the moment, so too could she begin to accept herself. As she was more able to reveal her terrible secrets and release them from the dungeons of her mind, so too could she begin to nurture the frightened little girl within.

It's easy to see that an experience like Carol's shakes the very foundation of a person's life. Forever after there is great difficulty feeling safe. Even when things seem to get better and the person leaves home and can no longer be threatened by family members, there is a feeling of dread. In order to even begin to talk about these early feelings, a person must feel absolutely safe. The person listening must be totally accepting and understanding, and must have worked through his or her own childhood feelings of abuse and abandonment in order to listen with compassion and care.

We often judge our past behavior by standards that were not present at the time the behavior occurred. We say to ourselves, for instance, I should have left sooner, or I shouldn't have come on romantically with that person. But when we take into account all the things that were true at the time, including our pain, our fear,

125

our rage, our hurt, we begin to see more clearly that we indeed did the best we could. We come to accept that, no matter how horrible our behavior may seem to us in retrospect, it was right, even necessary at the time. To accept our behavior in the past isn't to condone it or to make it all right to do again. Rather, this acceptance is needed to relieve us of the guilt and shame that keeps us locked in the past, repeating old and destructive patterns.

Once Carol could forgive herself and see herself as blameless, she could begin to move ahead and claim a more expansive future. Guilt and shame always keep us from accurately looking at our behavior and learning the lessons we need to learn in order to move ahead with our lives.

Carol began to see that she had, in many ways, re-created her family situation. Her husband was like the "good father" who didn't make love to his daughter. As a love partner, George turned her off. The other men in her life were like her "lascivious father." They were extremely exciting, but sleeping with them was forbidden and wrong. They were "family," the men in AA, the priest at her church.

Carol continues in therapy, seeing her sponsor regularly, and has expanded her involvement in AA. She recognizes that overcoming her alcoholism won't make her love addiction disappear. She continues to work on both.

"I'm Scared"

We think of abuse as being a conscious process. A parent actively and knowingly hurts a child. Yet most abuse is passive. The parent may not even be aware that the child was hurt. I still remember my own terror when my mother left me at home "for a few minutes" while she went to the store. As a four-year-old, I became frightened, then panicked, when it got dark and she wasn't home. I was sure she had left me and was never coming back. When she did return, probably not much later than she had said, I was crying uncontrollably in the front yard. She dried my tears and I'm sure forgot the incident. Forty years later I still shudder when it gets dark and someone I love is five minutes late.

Roger, the man we met in chapter 1, had to live with this passive kind of abuse. "My father died when I was eight and I still haven't gotten over it," he said in one of our early sessions. "We were very close and I loved him blindly and completely. We went everywhere together. One day we were planning to go to the store. He was in a hurry and left without me. An hour later we got a call from the sheriff that he had been in an accident and had died. I don't think I ever got over the loss or the feeling that if I had been with him he would have been driving more slowly and wouldn't have died."

The fear and insecurity resulting from these kinds of losses often are unresolved and deeply affect our lives, particularly our intimate relationships. Roger began to realize this during the course of therapy: "I'm starting to see that part of my obsession with women has to do with the loss I felt when my father died. It's like I need to have multiple partners because I still feel that someone close may die. Having multiple partners somehow protects me against the possible loss."

As Roger and I talked more he began to understand that no matter how many partners he had or how closely he held on to the ones he loved, he could never make up for his father's death or protect himself against further loss. Only by learning to accept the past and to deal realistically with the future could he hope to develop the stability and peace he was hoping to find.

To understand this endless search that people like Roger, Carol, and other love addicts are engaged in, we need to understand the basic human need for safety and security and the way in which these needs are undermined.

When We Don't Get What We Need

Dr. Abraham Maslow, a world-famous psychologist and authority on human development, tells us that there are certain needs that are shared by every human being.[1] It's obvious that we all need to have our physiological needs met if we are to survive as infants and later as adults. We need food and water or we soon perish. But Maslow suggested that we also need more than these; we need to feel safe and secure, to love and be loved and have a high level of self-esteem. Finally, Maslow feels that humans have a need for self-actualization, to become all that they are capable of becoming. If these needs are not met, we become sick in some way.

He suggested that these needs are arranged in a hierarchy, with physiological needs at the base and self-actualization needs at the top. A person who is lacking food, safety, love, and esteem would most probably hunger for food more strongly than for anything else. A person whose basic physiological needs have been met but is lacking safety, love, esteem, and self-actualization would hunger for safety more strongly than for anything else.

Love addicts are damaged at the level of safety and security. The drive to satisfy this need dominates their lives. It's why they are always looking for love in all the wrong places. They fail to recognize that until their needs for safety and security are met, they can never experience true love or feel a sense of their own worth and value as a human being. They continue to try and build relationships that require love, self-esteem, and self-actualization on a foundation that is missing a basic building block—safety and security—and thus their structures are forever falling down.

Pulitzer Prize–winning author and psychoanalyst Erik Erikson approaches the same issues from a slightly different perspective. He suggests, in his classic *Childhood and Society,* that each person passes through eight stages, each with specific tasks that must be accomplished and each with certain crises that must be confronted.[2]

The issues in the first stage of life have to do with basic trust vs. basic mistrust. For the infant to develop trust, his relationship with those who care for him must be based on consistency, continuity, and sameness of experience. As Erikson says, "Parents must not only have certain ways of guiding by prohibition and permission; they must also be able to represent to the child a deep, an almost somatic conviction that there is a meaning to what they are doing."[3]

This is exactly what is missing in the families many of us grew up in. Without the development of basic trust, safety, and security, the child continues to seek the fulfillment of these needs through all later stages.[4]

128

The Need For Safety and Security

In Part III, Getting Free, we will return to these themes and show that all successful addiction programs help restore basic trust and provide safety and security. They also help a person reconnect with their spiritual essence.

For now, let's examine more closely our need for safety and security since it is at the root of love addiction.

This need is often obscured in adults, but in infants we see clearly their obvious fearful reactions when they are suddenly disturbed or dropped, startled by loud noises, flashing lights, or other unusual sensory stimulation, by rough handling, by inadequate support or loss of support altogether.

As we pointed out in chapter 1, those of us who are love addicts come from families where safety and security needs were not met and where there was very little predictability. Dad may be loving one day. The next moment he is raging. Mom may give us the right degree of touch one day, the next she may be smothering or rejecting. As children we learn to survive in an environment that has no rules nor reason.

We desperately try to find something that is under our control. As children we learn to do the things that will elicit a supportive reaction from our parents. We also keep our world sane through fantasy. Later, drugs, alcohol, and romance become means we can use to give order to our world. They all start out as things that are under our control, that we can use to bring us pleasure and remove the pain we feel.

Another aspect of our need for safety and security is our preference for some kind of even rhythm in our lives. We want a predictable, orderly world. We never got that as children and we desperately seek it as adults.

Observing quarreling, physical assault, separation, divorce, or death are common experiences for us growing up. We also experience parental outbursts of rage and threats of punishment directed at us, name calling, being spoken to harshly, being handled roughly, or punished physically. The panic and terror we feel goes beyond

129

the fear of being hurt. Our worst fear is of being abandoned, a threat to our need for safety and security.

Children cling to abusive parents ever more tightly even when they have given up being loved, since more basic than being loved is our desire to feel secure. We often see that children who are terribly abused choose to return to their parents rather than going to live with strangers who are loving and who care. We see a similar pattern in adults who remain in abusive relationships.

Often we wonder why we stay in a relationship that is abusive. We think we must be crazy. I believe that we are not crazy at all but trying to meet our needs in the only way we know how. We stay in abusive relationships for two reasons. The first is that they are familiar. They feel "like home." The other reason is that we never give up trying to get our parents to take care of us. We continually re-create the same abusive situations we grew up in so we can try again and again to get the love we couldn't get while growing up.

Listen again to the words of people who have begun to recover from sex and love addictions as they describe the ways in which they attempted to meet their needs for security:

"I realized that when I was insecure I looked for some kind of romantic high to give me courage or calmness. I also realized that I was always playing some kind of romantic game. There was always a friend, or the wife of a friend, or a colleague, or a secretary or stewardess, or someone for whom I was on the make."

"I couldn't ever imagine a life without some kind of extra sex or romantic involvement. Even more important than the sex itself was the thrill of the chase, the high I would get when I would cruise my familiar haunts."

My own experience was much less traumatic than many love addicts and more subtle. My mother and father tried unsuccessfully to have a child over a period of fifteen years. When my mother became pregnant she was overjoyed and remembers "walking very carefully down Broadway, in New York, for fear of dislodging the baby."

After I was born she became obsessed with my health and safety. She said she wouldn't even let my father hold me or bathe me for

130

fear that I might get hurt. I was hers alone and only she could protect me.

With that feeling of fear, the kind of touching I got was often too close and smothering. I felt invaded. I grew up desperately wanting to connect with a woman, but needing to keep her at arm's length.

For love addicts, getting close is always fearful. Regardless of whether the abuse we receive is blatant or subtle, we begin to feel that life is not safe. To get the security that we crave in order to survive, we must become intimate with a parent who we cannot trust. Thus from the very beginning, intimacy is wrapped up with fear.

Although it may seem that love addicts are looking for more and more exciting sexual or romantic experiences, we are actually trying to fulfill our needs for safety and security while protecting ourselves against those we fear may harm us. We may seem to be the most mature adults, seeking the ultimate adult pleasures. But we are actually responding as scared children who never developed a firm enough base of security to be able to find real love and intimacy in the world.[5]

As children, some love addicts felt their very lives were threatened. Some were told that if they ever revealed the abuse, they would be killed. Most of us didn't fear for our physical lives, but were afraid we would be either abandoned or smothered emotionally. Since children are totally dependent on their parents, threats to safety and security needs are experienced in the same way as adults experience threats to their physical existence.

In order to develop a sense of security with people who act unpredictably and whom we cannot trust, we begin to develop elaborate means of gaining control over ourselves and others. This is the focus of the next chapter.

6. 'TIL DEATH DO US PART: Control at All Costs

Born to Rule

As children we were under the complete control of our parents. We knew that our security and sometimes our very lives depended on our satisfying their needs. We became hypersensitive to our parents. We learned to anticipate their moods, to "read" their body postures and expressions. We had to learn early what was expected of us in rapidly changing situations. We often shifted roles, from being the "child" to being the "parent" or "peacemaker." In order to survive we felt we needed to take control of those around us. We were always attempting to manage the actions of others. We also tried to manage our own feelings and desires in order to keep peace in the family. We felt responsible for our parents' drinking, anger, or unhappiness. We hoped that by controlling both our inner lives and the outer environment, we could make things right for them.

Recall the experiences of Roger. Control was a major issue in his early development, though it took him some time to recognize it. His family life alternated between extreme rigidity and chaos. For Roger, this was "normal." He described his family as very loving and supportive. His father had died when he was eight years old, but his mother took over and cared for him and his younger sister. "Mom did everything for us," he beamed with a proud smile. "We never wanted for anything."

As he described his "loving mother," I found myself becoming increasingly uncomfortable. "My Mom was a stickler for order. In fact she still is." Roger chuckled. "Everything has a place and she gets very upset if things are moved. She organizes her closets so that dresses, blouses, coats, and shoes are arranged by color and fabric. Every bowl and ashtray has a place, every magazine must sit just so.

"When we got up in the morning she picked out our clothes, helped us to dress and tied our shoes. . . . She was always afraid we would do it wrong." He paused and turned his head thoughtfully. "She did that every day until we were ten or eleven." His look seemed to say, What sacrifice, what love!

The only break in his description of total admiration for this "saint" of a mother was when he described his day. "She'd send us off to school and it was a long walk, sometimes in the snow. It was like—like, when we were home she was doing everything for us. But once we were out of the house she didn't seem to notice us." He looked a little puzzled as he recalled the experience, but his tone and description still seemed to say, But, this is the way families are, so it must be right.

He again seemed slightly puzzled, but no less accepting, when he recalled a number of times when he and his sister were cold. "I remember one day, it must have been well below zero, and I had forgotten my mittens. I knocked on the window for a long time, but Mom didn't come. Finally, she appeared and in a calm voice told us 'Stay out and play now, it isn't time to come in.' I was freezing, but I felt ashamed that I had bothered her."

As I listened to him I thought how unconsciously he had re-created the experience in his family home. Lacking control as a boy growing up, he had created a family situation in adulthood that was very similar to the one in which he was raised. His wife seemed withdrawn and indifferent, like his "stay-out-and-play" mother, while his young lover fawned over him totally, like his "I'll-tie-your-shoes" mother. The crucial difference was that now as an adult he felt in control of the situation.

Our supersensitivity seems to serve us well as adults. It's the reason many love addicts make such good therapists and counselors. Our ability to know what others are feeling is almost bred in our bones. This ability often makes us extremely attractive as romantic partners. We seem so loving, so caring, so understanding.

The real issue for us, however, is control. The reason there are so many love addicts in the helping professions, in politics, and at the executive levels of business is that we are drawn to positions in which we can exercise a high degree of power.

We begin to see the importance of control for the love addict when we observe how tenaciously we try to hold on to it in our relationships and how frightened and upset we become when we begin to lose it.

Carol remembered the ways she tried to control people in her life. "I used to call my friend three and four times a day. It was like I had to continually reassure myself that he was there. If he was gone and didn't return my call when I expected him to, I would get panicked. At first I would fly into a rage, then I would break down in tears. I felt like I was losing my grip on things. The more I tried to hold on to people, the more they seemed to move away from me. The more I tried to control things, the more out of control they became."

The 3 C's Revisited

Roger also experienced the "3 C's" associated with addictions—Compulsion, loss of Control, and Continued involvement despite problems. Although his relationship with his girlfriend, Laura, was endangering his marriage and had contributed to the loss of a number of jobs, he felt unable to stop seeing her.

Trying to change his behavior through willpower only seemed to make things worse. As he said, "I've always seen myself as a strong man, able to do anything if I set my mind to it. But this thing with Laura is different. I can't seem to stop seeing her even

135

though I want to. I'm able to stay away from her for a few weeks. I was even able to stay away for three months once. But just when I think I've taken control of things, I remember her smile or something we did together and I'm on my way to her house. I almost feel like I'm hypnotized. Some force just seems to drive me back to her. I tried for eighteen years to quit smoking cigarettes. I finally succeeded. I feel like I'm more hooked on Laura than I was on nicotine and it terrifies me that I might never be able to stop."

Since loss of control is such a key issue for love addicts, as it is for other addicts, let's look at this issue in greater depth.

In studying alcoholism, for example, loss of control is seen by most experts as the key element that distinguishes those who are addicted from those who are not.[1] Alcoholics begin by feeling that alcohol is a friend. They drink and they like it. Later they begin to have some problems, but feel they can control their drinking by cutting back, drinking only on weekends, or giving up the "hard stuff." As they find they cannot consistently control their drinking, they begin to rationalize their behavior. "Why should I limit my drinking to weekends? I like a beer after work." "I can handle scotch, it's just bourbon that causes me problems." Finally, they become completely unable to control their drinking, but without help continue to deny the situation. As their lives become more unmanageable the effects of drinking become overwhelmingly destructive.

One of the difficulties in getting an addict to accept help is the belief that all of us should be able to control our behavior. This is particularly true with men, whose conditioning has been that being a man and being in control are almost synonymous. To accept that we are addicted, that we are no longer able to control our behavior, feels like the loss of our very identity as a human being.

Admitting We're Powerless

Every addict clings to these two beliefs: 1. I can control my drinking (drugging, smoking, gambling, overeating, promiscuity); 2. I am not an addict. Recovery begins when the person can say: 1. I cannot control my drinking (drugging, smoking, gambling, overeating, promiscuity); 2. I am an addict.

The first step in all 12-step programs of recovery is the acknowledgment that we are powerless over our addictions, whatever form they take. The second step involves accepting that there is something or someone, some power greater than ourselves, that can help us.

Those of us who have become addicted are in a real bind. We gradually become aware that our behaviors have become compulsive. We see how preoccupied we have become with our addictive relationship. We may even accept that we have lost control and that we are powerless over our addiction. We try everything possible to make things better but finally accept that we just make things worse. We often get a sober glimpse into our future and see that we can't make things better on our own, that we need another human being to help guide us.

This realization is terrifying, since we believe that our survival has depended on our being able to make our own way in the world. Now, having lost trust in our ability to take care of ourselves, the thought of placing our trust in someone else feels suicidal, and triggers feelings from our long forgotten past. Is it any wonder that we desperately cling to any vestige of belief that we can still control our addiction?

Love becomes an addiction when we use it to cover our pain and fill the void we feel inside. The addictive process stems from our desire to feel whole, to have control over our own lives. In this respect addictions are based on the universal human need to feel complete and autonomous; their underlying motivation is therefore positive. But as our addictions become ever more destructive, we often feel there is an "evil" core at the very center of our being that must be destroyed even if we die in the process. It can be lifesaving for the addict to know that this is not true: At the very center of our being is simply a legitimate desire for wholeness and love. Our addictive beliefs and behaviors were the best way we knew at the time to survive in the world and meet our needs.

We don't have to destroy the center of our being in order to keep our addictions from killing us.

137

This revelation saved my life. I had spent a lifetime running away from myself, trying desperately to fill the void I felt inside. When I realized that I couldn't keep running, I thought my only hope was to somehow cut out that terrible core. I often had dreams about what life would be like if I had to cut out my own heart in order to survive. It took a long time before I began to trust that there was another way.

In order to understand this process we must first identify the ways in which we have tried, unsuccessfully, to control our world. We will see that our compulsive search for love and romance was our way of trying to gain control over our world. We will find that in our attempt to control those around us, we have lost even more control over ourselves. Finally, we will come to understand that it is our desire to control the world that is killing us. Only by acknowledging our lack of control can we take the first steps toward recovery.

The 7 Stages of Romantic and Sexual Addictions

Since love addiction evolves slowly, over a long period of time, it is difficult to understand it at any moment. Let's follow one person through the entire process.

STAGE 1

Jack was a beautiful baby. Labor had lasted almost twenty-four hours, but the delivery went smoothly. When baby Jack took his first breath and the cord was cut he became fully alive. Like all human beings, he had to separate from the warmth and comfort inside his mother's body, where all his needs were met instantly. Yet separation also brought with it the opportunity to learn to re-relate—first to mother, then to the rest of the world—as a complete human being. From the moment of birth Jack was complete and perfect. He had all that was required to become the person he was meant to be. Just as the oak tree is contained in the acorn, his whole life was contained in the fertilized seed that was his personal blueprint.

Yet the process is never perfect. Jack, like all human beings, came into an imperfect world. His parents were young and had never fully developed their own lives. Their angers, hurts, fears, guilt, and shame were all passed on to him. Rather than understanding that his parents were incomplete and not perfect beings, he came to believe that there was something missing in him, something that could be filled only from outside.

STAGE 2

As a child Jack was a happy kid. He felt terrible when his parents fought and did everything he could to make them happy. He didn't know that Dad's drinking had escalated or that Dad's angry outbursts were caused by personal problems; he assumed they happened because he hated Jack. Jack and his mother took solace in each other. He loved the way she rubbed his back when he was hurt. He learned early that a woman's touch could brighten his world when it grew dim, could make him feel whole again when he was shattered.

As a young boy he was shy and withdrawn. He didn't make friends easily and spent hours fantasizing how much he would love to touch all the pretty girls in his class. He snuck his first drink at a New Year's Eve party when he was eleven and felt safe and powerful for the first time in his life. His early sexual fantasies and his bottle became special friends that seemed to fill the hole that was growing inside him.

STAGE 3

As Jack got older these "friends" became more and more important in his life. When we substitute alcohol and sexual fantasies for the real experiences of becoming friends with ourselves and the people in our lives, our development becomes arrested. We get older, but we don't mature.

Jack continued to seek out those experiences that seemed to bring him instant pleasure and relief from the pain and loneliness that were his everyday companions. It felt so good to have friends you

139

could really count on, who would always be there for you, available at the tip of a glass or through a glance at a magazine.

But he still felt lonely and was becoming increasingly depressed. His job as a checker at the local supermarket paid well, but wasn't very satisfying. He found it very difficult to meet women, though he had constant fantasies about customers and other employees. When Sharon invited him out for a drink after work, he was flustered but jumped at the chance. When he didn't follow up their first date, she did. They were married the following summer in a private ceremony with two people from the market as their witnesses.

He hoped that marriage would fill the void he felt and replace his increasing dependency on alcohol and sexual fantasy. For the first two years that seemed to be the case. But when their son was born, Jack felt scared again. He had recurring dreams that Sharon would take their son and leave him. She continued to love Jack as before, though she also loved their new son, and couldn't understand why Jack seemed to withdraw.

He began to drink more, spent evenings going to pornographic movies alone, and began following pretty women on the street. Once again he hoped he had filled the void inside. His fears of abandonment faded into the background.

STAGE 4

But rather than filling him up and satisfying his needs for security, love, and affection, these activities actually left him feeling even more empty inside. He blamed Sharon for his unhappiness and accused her of caring more for the baby than she did for him. Coming home drunk one night after flirting with a woman at work, feeling ashamed and guilty, he and Sharon got into a fight. For the first time in their marriage Jack slapped his wife, hard enough to knock her down.

They both cried afterward and he swore it would never happen again. He blamed it on his drinking and promised he would cut back or stop altogether. When he hit Sharon an image flashed through his memory; he remembered the many times he had been

140

slapped by his father. He had vowed that he would never grow up to be like his father and was horrified to think that he might have become just the same.

By the next morning he had all but forgotten the incident. Only Sharon's black eye, almost covered by added makeup, gave him a vague reminder that something had happened. He did know that he had to get control of himself. He decided he would cut down on his drinking and stay away from pretty women.

But the more he tried to control his behavior, the more his mind became preoccupied. He began to fantasize ever more bizarre and violent situations. He would hide pornographic magazines in his locker at work and take them into the bathroom to look at. After returning to his cash register he felt curiously peaceful. But the peace was short-lived and his work breaks became more frequent. His supervisor called him in and told him he was a valued employee but that he couldn't continue to take so many breaks during his shift.

Jack seemed to be losing control over his life. The harder he tried to fix things, the worse they got. In his panic and fear, he now blamed his wife for the problems he was having at work and blamed his supervisor at work for the problems he was having with Sharon. Only his old "friends" never criticized him, never disappointed him, never made him wait.

Ever since an early time in his life Jack felt like only half a person. Somewhere there must be a partnership that will make me whole, he thought. One half plus one half equals one. But every partnership he found (with alcohol, sex, or even Sharon) seemed to leave him emptier than before.

The more we seek to fill our missing part by looking outside ourselves, the less complete we become. Yet the more empty we feel the more inclined we are to seek out our addictions. The more Jack tried to fill himself up, the smaller he became.

STAGE 5

As the cycle continued Jack felt locked onto a treadmill whose speed kept increasing. The faster he ran, the more he seemed to fall

141

behind. He lost his job. Though he found another one, the stress at home increased and the new job paid less money.

Afraid Sharon would leave him, a terrifying possibility, he made herculean efforts to control his drinking. Sharon knew nothing about Jack's fantasy life; all she could see were the problems alcohol was causing.

Proud that he now had his drinking under control, Jack often felt deprived of its comfort. As his drinking receded into the background, his love life became more active and more chaotic—he had substituted one addiction for another. His new job as a salesman kept him on the road a lot and afforded him the freedom to pursue his sexual fantasies.

He was beginning to suspect that he had a romantic addiction. But since it was easier for him to see problems in others rather than in himself, he began to notice other people who drank too much, ate compulsively, or gambled their money away. As he got to know some of these people and listened to them talk about their romantic exploits and fantasies, he suspected increasingly that many alcoholics, food addicts, and their spouses also had a more hidden addiction—love addiction—at the core of their being.

STAGE 6

Jack's inkling that he might be addicted to fantasy and romantic intrigue was frightening. To even think such thoughts might mean that he would have to get help. But "help" for Jack felt like death. To give up the only thing in his life that gave him pleasure, that protected him from the depression and guilt that often overwhelmed him, was unthinkable.

As the cycle of addiction became ever more destructive, his denial that he had a problem became more entrenched. Afraid to tell anyone about this hidden part of his life, he became more isolated from those around him. Even his social life with Sharon became more restricted. He didn't want to see friends and would go to parties only if he was sure there would be women he could fantasize about.

142

He literally became lost in the world of romantic intrigue and acting out. His only friends now were his fantasy lovers. Even though they were causing his life to become more narrow and unmanageable, he clung to them like a drowning man clings to a life preserver. Jack was like a prisoner who falls in love with his captors.

STAGE 7

Jack was dying. The addiction was killing him. Yet in his tortured mind, he hoped against hope that things would get better without his having to give up his fantasy lovers. And in truth, there were times when things seemed to improve. He would play with his son and feel that life was worth living. His wife would hug him and tell him everything was going to be all right.

But the moments of joy only served to keep him hooked on his self-destructive addiction. Like a laboratory rat that only gets re-warded once every 300 times, he lived for the hope of reward. It didn't take much to convince him that things were okay, that he didn't need to change.

When Sharon found out about his sexual fantasizing, having discovered a whole drawerful of pornography, Jack felt terrified but also relieved. At least someone else knew. But he still refused to seek help and once again alternated between angry outbursts at his wife and solitary times with his fantasy rituals.

In the past he had refused to seek help because he didn't want to change. Now he felt he couldn't change. He knew he was addicted to love, but he also felt there was no hope. Once an addict, always an addict, he thought. He was sure his family would be better off without him.

He had always been afraid of guns, but he liked the feel of the small pistol he had purchased from a pawnshop not far from home. It seemed so smooth in his hand. The bullets were so soft, almost friendly, as he slid them into the chamber. He slid the end of the barrel into his mouth. It tasted cold.

143

The Paradox of Control

I've known too many people who have gone through the seven stages of this tragic play. But I've known many more who recognized the ending before it was too late.

The paradox of control is simple. The more we try to control life, the more we are in danger of losing it. Our fears tell us that we must hold on to survive. Instead, we must learn to trust enough to know when to let go. The Japanese say that in a storm it is the bamboo, the flexible tree that can bend with the wind, that survives. The rigid tree that resists the wind falls.

To become more like the bamboo, we must understand our addictive relationships and return to the world of our parents. Bill and Sandra will be our guides as we explore the world of addicted lovers and revisit Mom and Dad in the next chapter.

7. ADDICTED LOVERS: Mom and Dad Revisited

"We Fight All the Time"

Bill and Sandra were referred to me by another therapist. When Sandra called she said she and her husband were looking for someone who specialized in working with couples and who also understood addictions.

She was a striking woman. Her loosely tied long red hair and deep blue eyes made her look much younger than thirty-eight. She was friendly on first meeting, but seemed to be holding back a tremendous amount of feeling. When she stopped smiling her face took on an altogether different appearance. There were two deep furrows between her eyebrows that gave her an angry, judgmental look.

Bill seemed shy when we first met. He looked sad and slightly frightened. Where Sandra filled the room with her energy, he gave the appearance of wanting to hide his own.

"We've been together three years," Sandra began, taking charge of the silence after introductions were made. "And things have gotten so bad between us we fight all the time." I could certainly picture her fighting. As I looked at her long, bright red fingernails,

I felt she was the type who wouldn't hesitate to use them as weapons if she felt threatened. It was more difficult to imagine Bill losing his temper, though I've known many quiet types who can be quite dangerous when they finally blow up.

"I'm not even sure what we fight about anymore," she continued. "But if we can't work things out soon, I know I want to get out of the marriage and get on with my life." Bill's eyes widened in response, but he didn't say anything. He seemed to withdraw more deeply into the chair and I imagined that his heart was pounding faster.

Over the next few sessions their story unfolded. Both had been married twice before and they entered their third marriage with a great deal of passion for each other, but also fear about the future. They spent months developing a marriage contract that spelled out their love for each other, the ways they would treat the children from previous marriages, their goals, their financial plans, and a detailed description of how they would dissolve their union in the event that things did not work out between them. One of the agreements they had made was to see a therapist if they could not resolve things on their own. They were keeping their agreement by coming to see me.

Sandra's main complaint centered around her fear of Bill's infidelity. His was that she criticized him constantly and that her fears of his infidelity were groundless. I got a flavor of their interaction in one of the early sessions.

"I know you, Bill. I see you looking at all those women. I thought you were different, but you're just like all the other chauvinist bastards I know. You shit, you . . ." Sandra went on nonstop for over ten minutes. I watched Bill's face redden and his fists clench until he finally exploded. He groped for words, but his feelings were explosive. "God damn you . . . You . . . God damn you . . . you bitch! What do you expect me to do? You're always on me, you never give me any peace. When I look at you all I see is hatred and disgust in your eyes. I'm not looking at other women. I'm just trying to look at anyone but you!"

I thought it would be useful to see the couple separately for a while. I wanted to understand them better individually and I had

146

some real concerns that their explosive interactions might lead to violence, either after the sessions or even during.

What We Learned from Our Parents

In talking with each of them, they revealed a history of abuse and abandonment that had gone back generations. Sandra had been abused by her father and her grandmother during the first six or seven years of her life. She revealed these experiences very slowly and reluctantly, even though she had been in therapy for five years after the breakup of her first marriage.

She said she had touched on the abuse, but never in depth and had never told the whole story. "Actually," she said, "I'm not even sure I know the whole story. Each time I dig deeper I seem to find more. Memories that seemed buried beneath the sand at the bottom of the deepest ocean float to the surface. Just when I think I've gotten them all, another one appears."

Her mother and father fought a great deal. After coming home drunk once and finding the dinner dishes still in the sink, her dad broke her mom's jaw and whipped the children. The next day when he went to work Sandra, her younger brother, and their mother left to stay with their mother's mother in Florida.

"I was so glad to get away from my father," Sandra recalled. "I thought anyplace would be better. I was wrong. My mom got a job as a waitress while she took acting classes in the evening and left me and my brother Bobby with my grandmother. She never hurt us physically, but she beat us down emotionally. She would yell at us and threaten to whip us. I wanted so much for her to like me, but nothing I ever did pleased her. She said I was bad, that I had gotten it from my father. I truly felt that I was bad in the bone. Strange as it seemed, I missed my father and remembered the good times we had and forgot the bad.

"It took me a long time to talk to my mother. I think Bobby and I were both scared to say anything. My grandmother said no one would believe us if we told. We were bad children. I guess I believed her. When I finally told my mother how frightened we were, she just said it would be okay, that grandma loved us and wouldn't do

147

anything to hurt us. I felt trapped. Bobby retreated into fantasy. I retreated into music. The only time my grandmother let me alone was when I was playing the piano."

Bill's story was different in detail but similar in the abuse and abandonment that had gone back generations. He described his father as "the most loving and kind man I've ever known." He died when Bill was eleven and it was a loss that he still mourned almost thirty years later. "My dad," he said with a glow on his face, "was a truckdriver. He was big and rough, but when he would pick me up and put me on his shoulders his touch was as light as the wind. He'd take me with him on some of his trips and I loved to sit up in the cab. I felt so powerful, like I could do anything as long as Dad was with me. I met other truckers, friends of his, on the road. They called him 'Big Mike,' I never knew why, and me 'Little Mike.' I was just so proud to be with him.

"When he died things weren't the same again. Mom had to go out to work. She had never been very independent. She loved to stay at home and take care of me. She didn't even know how to drive. Dad's heart attack came without warning and she had to learn fast so she could keep us afloat. She never talked about Dad's death, just as she had never talked about any feelings. It was understood that big boys don't cry and I should take my loss like a man. It was funny. I always thought of my father as the nurturing mother figure and my mother as man-of-the-house.

"I tried to take over for Dad. I got a job delivering papers and was always getting beaten up by older kids in the neighborhood. I remember coming home in tears when they took all my money after I had made my collection. It was the first time I had ever seen Mom drunk. She and Dad used to have wine with dinner and they both drank beer when we'd have picnics on warm summer days. But that day I came home, Mom was sitting with a bottle of vodka. All thoughts of my own pain vanished and I just wanted to take care of her. I helped her upstairs and got her undressed. She wanted me to lie down beside her. We'd never been that close physically. She always seemed distant, and I felt uncomfortable. But I lay with her and she finally fell asleep.

"Well, the drinking increased and when she was drunk she always

148

wanted me to sit or lie down with her. She wanted me to rub her shoulders and sometimes she would rub my back, which I loved. She began rubbing down my body and I remember feeling so embarrassed that I got an erection. She just said it was okay, not to worry. I liked her touch, but I was revolted at the same time. I wanted to run out of the room, but I didn't want to hurt her feelings. When I did try to leave she would get mean and nasty. I decided it was better to do what she wanted."

As Bill and Sandra filled me in more about their own growing up we began to see the connection to their present situation. Both of them were abused children whose parents were also abused children. They each grew up having to deal with the loss of a father, which I have found is a common experience for people who become addicts. It is often within the family that we first develop the patterns that later become addictive.

Our first experiences with intimacy take place in our families. Our first lovers are our mothers and fathers. The beliefs about safety, sexuality, love, and intimacy that develop early form the basis for our adult relationships.

It is too simple to say, as some have, that all men marry their mothers and all women marry their fathers. But it is true that in searching for an intimate partner, we are driven by the fears and desires that we acquired from the first great loves of our lives— Mom and Dad.

Without being aware of it, we often repeat experiences that we had as small children. We find partners who evoke the same mixture of fear and hope that was present with our parents.

As we discussed in previous chapters, one of the basic beliefs that infuses the lives of love addicts is that we *must* find someone to hook onto in order to survive. Yet the more we search for that needed other the farther away we get from the source of our own redemption, ourselves.

What You Already Know

An addiction exists when a person's attachment to a sensation, an object, or another person is such as to lessen his appreciation of and ability to deal with other things in his environment or in himself. The person becomes increasingly dependent on that experience as his only source of gratification.

In order to break the destructive belief system, we have to recognize it. As we do so, we begin to become less a victim and more in control of our own lives. In order to release ourselves from being victims, we must shine the light of our vision and understanding on the beliefs we acquired from our parents.

This involves a process of remembering experiences that we long ago buried because they were so painful. As children, we had to "forget" the pain of being abused or we would surely have become psychotic or suicidal. As adults we must return to the world of our parents in order to recover and free ourselves.

This process involves two stages. The first is to reexperience our pain, to acknowledge to ourselves the reality of our abuse and the ways those early experiences have directed our lives. It involves a great deal of courage and willingness to go into the darkest recesses of our psyches. For many of us it means going into hell.

Like Bill and Sandra we remember small fragments of events at first, but often our feelings are not connected to the events. We've buried the emotions that went with the experience. Later the emotions begin to flood out. Our fear is that we will drown in the feelings. We need to trust that we will remember only what we are ready to handle and we can move at our own speed.

Once we are able to move beneath our shell of emotional numbness we find even more buried feelings. Behind a person who is numb is an angry person. When we are able to accept and express our anger, we are drawn down to the next level. After the anger comes the hurt. We feel once again the pain of the abuse and cry the tears that were often withheld as we grew up.

I have found that some people first experience anger and are later able to experience the hurt, while others first become aware of the hurt and later experience the anger. Whichever comes first, the next level that people feel is their fear. We remember the terror we felt as helpless children trying to deal with parents who were often irrational and hurtful.

When we learn to express our fear and come to accept these

150

feelings, we drop down another layer and experience guilt and shame. We often think of guilt and shame as being the same emotion, yet there is a subtle but important difference between them.

Guilt is the feeling we get when we have failed to live up to some inner standard. We may feel guilty when we cheat on our wives or lie to our parents. It is a fault of *doing*. The result is we feel wicked. Shame also involves feeling bad, but it results when we feel exposed. It's like a bright light shining on us, showing the whole world how worthless we are. Shame is a more debilitating emotion since it tells us that we have failed in *being*.

All of us who have experienced love addictions feel very guilty about what we've done. We need to learn to make amends for our actions. The more difficult task is to learn to feel good about ourselves once again. This involves learning to overcome our shame. The process begins when we are able to experience and express the five emotions described above.[1]

It's easy to talk about feelings, easy to say that in order to heal we need to experience our anger, hurt, fear, guilt, and shame. It's much more difficult to do it. It can help to know that the feelings are there, though often they seem buried so deeply we can't believe we have them.

Once we have expressed these emotions we can return to the center of our being, where we experience love and understanding. Most of us who are addicts are convinced that at the center of our being we are bad or, worse, that we are empty. It takes a long time to find out that our natural state is one of love.

Learning Forgiveness

The second stage of revisiting our childhood is to move beyond our own abuse to see that our parents were also abused children. If we see our parents only as oppressors, we remain stuck in our anger, hurt, or fear. When we can glimpse what their lives were like, we can understand and learn to forgive them. Only through forgiving others can we heal ourselves.

As a child Sandra saw her grandmother as merely another person who was abusing her. During her therapy she began to see that

151

this was the person who had nurtured her mother when her mother was a little girl. As Sandra talked with her mother she came to realize that her mother too had been abused and molested when she was a little girl. Her grandfather had abandoned the family when her mother was young.

Bill began to see similar patterns as he explored how the world looked to his parents when they were children. He found that he had come from a long line of absent fathers. A number had died young. His mother had grown up in a household where both parents were absent and she was cared for by an aunt who was hooked on alcohol and was physically and emotionally abusive.

One recovering love addict, Doris, remembered the following: "I was always treated like someone's plaything. I had a mind of my own and wanted my parents to see that. Yet they always told me how sweet and cute I was. I felt like a doll. I was theirs to do with as they pleased. For my mother, it was to take care of me when she felt like it and ignore me most of the time. For my father it was to fondle me when he was drunk and amorous, and beat me when he was drunk and mean. My basic belief about life was that I survived by making myself available to be played with. The more like a plaything I became, the more I could count on surviving, but the more I had to kill off my feelings and become the 'doll' others wanted."

As Doris began to reexperience the reality of her early life, she became extremely angry. She would have bouts of murderous rage, releasing the years of hatred that had built up. Below the anger were layers and layers of hurt and pain.

When she worked through the painful experiences, she had to deal with her fears—fear that she would be abandoned, fear that she would never be attractive enough to hold on to a man, and fear that the only way she could be intimate was to kill off the vital centers of her soul.

Underneath the fear, she discovered a reservoir of guilt. "Although I knew it was irrational, I felt I was to blame for the way I was treated. Somehow I felt that if it weren't for me, my parents would be happy. They wouldn't fight and my father wouldn't drink.

152

There were times when my father touched me that I liked the feelings. I felt ashamed and guilty."

As she reexperienced the feelings she was able to begin to understand what her parents' lives were like. The first glimmer of understanding led her to want to know more about her parents' childhood development. Her father had been beaten repeatedly by an uncle and had almost died from being hit with a horsewhip. He had joined the Marines and served valiantly in World War II. He never seemed to recover from being dishonorably discharged for hitting an officer who had called him a "sissy."

Doris's mother was the child of a heroin addict. She was born addicted and had to be given drugs just to keep her from dying from heroin withdrawal. She too became an addict when she was old enough to sell her body to get a fix.

Once Doris was able to express her feelings and forgive herself for being "bad," she could also see her parents more clearly and forgive them for her mistreatment. Healing can only come when we "let it flow, and let it go." It takes many years to build up our feelings and it takes years for us to release them. The process is difficult, but not impossible. The only alternative is increasing descent into the destructive spiral of addiction.

In my own case, it was a revelation for me to realize that my mother had been abandoned by her father when she was seven or eight, just as my father had left us and I had left my own children after a painful divorce.

My mother married four times. I was shocked to find out about the first marriage (my father was her second husband) when she mentioned it casually when I was thirteen. As an adult I always heard stories from my aunt about my parents' sexual and romantic intrigues.

As I learned more about abuse and addiction I searched my family history to understand the patterns that had been passed down from one generation to the next. I found that our family history was full of stories of abandonment, abuse, and sexual exploits and exploitation.

Until we recognize the abuse and addiction and make a conscious decision to heal ourselves, we will pass on our pain and self-destructive urges to the next generation. No matter how often we resolve to "treat my kids better than my parents treated me," we will "do unto them what was done to us." The only hope is that we recognize the abuse and begin a process of self-healing.

Beyond Family Stereotypes

In helping clients look back over the generations, I discovered two common experiences that surprised me. The first was the amount of abuse—physical, emotional, and sexual—enacted by women. The second was the predominance of absent fathers.

I grew up feeling that it was men who were brutal. What is clear from looking back on my own history, however, and that of many of my clients is that both men and women abuse children. This isn't surprising when we recognize that we pass on the abuse we experience as children. If we are abused, we will grow up to be abusers.

The stories of absent fathers seem almost universal in the lives of love addicts. Men are often portrayed as selfish brutes who abandon their families because they are too irresponsible and uncaring to stay and nurture them. Yet the truth is that many fathers "abandon" their families by dying young. We sympathize with a single mother left to care for small children, but often forget to ask about the stress and pain that leads so many men to die before their time.

When a man and woman divorce and she is left with the children, our concern usually goes toward "her and the kids." We rarely wonder about his side of the story. Yet as I've spoken to more and more men who have been able to open themselves up, many have spoken of their fear of staying close to those they love. A number of them said that they left their families to protect them against their own violence. One man I worked with, looking back on his divorce, had this to say: "What women don't seem to understand is that I close myself down because I'm afraid of hurting them, not because I don't love them. When I left my wife and little girl, it

154

was because I felt they would be better off without me, not because I didn't care."

Children suffer when parents remove themselves from the scene. Nevertheless, we don't make things better by beating up on men who leave. Most already feel bad enough. We can break the cycle of self-loathing and guilt by helping men deal with their anger and pain and by helping them understand how important they are in the lives of their children.

We've often focused on the importance of fathers to the growth and development of their sons, but time after time women tell me about the tremendous loss they felt when their fathers left the family. Experts are just now beginning to recognize the importance of the father-daughter bond. Although clinicians since Freud have emphasized the mother-child relationship, fathers are extremely important, particularly in the lives of their daughters. Dr. William Appleton, Assistant Clinical Professor of Psychiatry at Harvard Medical School, notes that a healthy father-daughter bond is most important during the difficult stage when the girl is moving from childhood to adolescence.[2]

Appleton says it's surprising that fathers affect their daughters' femininity more than their sons' masculinity. Contrary to popular belief, it's the father rather than the mother who's crucial in helping his daughter develop a healthy sex and love life. A good relationship with a warm and accepting father who is not too frightened of her sexuality is necessary for normal development in a girl. I believe many of the women who grow up to be love addicts are still searching for the warmth and acceptance of a missing father.

When we are able to heal our own wounds, forgive our parents, and recognize that we are all wounded children of wounded parents, we take another step in understanding our addiction and getting free.

PART III

Getting Free

8. HOW TO OVERCOME LOVE ADDICTIONS

"People Can Trust Me Now"

It's been seven years since Kevin first walked into my office. He's now married for the second time, happy he says for the first time in his life. His psychotherapy practice, once in shambles because he continued to become romantically involved with clients, now flourishes.

Sitting in my office having returned for one of our twice-yearly "fine-tuning" sessions, Kevin looks younger than his forty-three years. He seems content and relaxed as he reflects on the years of torment before he came for treatment and the difficult process of treatment itself.

"You know the thing that stands out for me," he says quietly, "is that people can trust me now." He stretches out his long legs. "I never could understand why people would come to me for help and then leave abruptly. I thought I was covering my lust so well. I never felt clean inside and I guess people picked that up. Now there are few inconsistencies between what's going on inside and what I express on the outside. Things aren't perfect, I don't expect they ever will be, but it's wonderful to know that people are safe around me."

One of the advantages of being a therapist for close to twenty-five years is that I can see people's progress over a long period of time. When I was just starting out in the field, I was sure addictions could be "cured" in a year or two at the most. I was also naive enough and arrogant enough to believe that the recovery process began when the person first came into my office. Prior to that magic moment the person was "sick," after it he or she was on a steady path to health and well-being.

Everything changed for me when I recognized that I had chosen, without being aware of it, to work with addictions because that was the problem I needed to work on in myself. The founders of the 12-step programs believed that everyone is both the helper and the one needing help. It's been a tremendous burden on "professional" helpers that our training has often taught us to deny our own needs.

"I've told you," Kevin says with a smile, "that your help was absolutely crucial to my recovery. There was even a time when I didn't think I could survive without your support. But looking back on things now, I can see that there were so many people who were crucial to my recovery. At the time, I was so angry and afraid all I could see were people who didn't give a damn about me.

"One of the greatest gifts I ever received was my first wife telling me she loved me, but couldn't live with me another day. I never believed she'd do it, but the next day she left, taking my son and daughter with her. I cried for weeks and hated the friends who came by to comfort me. I'll never forget Matt, the only friend who wouldn't put up with my sniveling after I'd drink myself into oblivion and wake up hung over the next day. His words were tough, but they were also loving and they jarred me out of the self-pity I was lost in. 'Kevin, I love you too much to watch you kill yourself. I'm going to an AA meeting tonight. I'll pick you up at six, and if you aren't ready to go, you can look for another friend.' " Kevin's eyes filled with tears as he remembered Matt. "You know he died of cancer, don't you? He was just fifty. He overcame his alcoholism

160

and helped so many others, but couldn't kick his addiction to cigarettes. I still miss him."

When I first met Kevin, he had been in AA for three years. Though his 12-step program had enabled him to turn his life around, his love addiction continued untreated.

Kevin's story was similar to that of many love addicts I had treated over the years, though it was also unique. From the time Kevin was three he said he knew something was wrong with his father. He would often have mood swings, being full of energy for weeks, expansive, ecstatically happy and very talkative, and then shift to times of depression, moodiness, and utter silence. Kevin said he never knew when the shift was going to happen, and the uncertainty was more terrifying than the actual episodes.

During the time I saw Kevin he began to sort out how his father's behavior had affected him. "I was an only child and before my dad got sick, he used to spend a great deal of time with me. When he changed, I retreated into a world of fantasy. It seemed so much safer and more predictable to have friends I could trust. The world of fantasy became more real to me than anything outside. While my dad alternated between states of manic excitement and withdrawn moodiness, I would happily talk to my imaginary playmates.

"I think I discovered sensuality when I was six or seven. I used to play house with a little girl who lived in the neighborhood. We had vivid imaginations and would create elaborate scenes of family life. We didn't know about sex, at least consciously, but we played the kind of games kids play at that age. From then on, romantic fantasy began to consume my waking thoughts and occupy my dreams.

"By the time I was eleven I spent hours reading romantic novels my mother had in her bedroom. No one ever found out or cared to get close enough to ask. Pornography was much less available, but I always managed to steal a nudist magazine from the newsstand, take it home, and create elaborate fantasies.

"I fell in love and married the girl I met my first day of college and though we were happy for a long time my romantic preoccupation never left me. As my behavior got more and more out of control, I began to drink heavily.

161

"The only other thing that even came close to matching the thrill of sexual excitement was my desire to become a therapist. Ever since watching Dr. Welby on television, I knew I wanted to become a doctor who talked to people about their problems. On some unconscious level I'm sure I also wanted to help my father. I found I was a natural helper and easily got through graduate school. I quickly transferred my romantic obsession to my clients. It was easy for them to fall in love with me and it was easy for me to lead them on and still tell myself that I wasn't doing anything wrong.

"I know the thing that saved my life, oddly enough, was when my wife left me and I was forced to confront my problems. It's been a long road, but I know it was necessary. I feel free and safe for the first time in my life. I don't have to save my dad and I don't have to hide from myself."

A Program for Recovery

After taking hundreds of people like Kevin through the process of recovery, I have evolved a 12-step system that fits my own understanding of what works and has been helpful to the people who have sought me out. It's certainly not the only system for helping people addicted to love, but I offer it as a roadmap for others to follow. As is true of any map, it only symbolically represents the actual terrain. The steps are never so logical and discrete in real life. No one ever follows them in order from beginning to end. Even arranging them in numerical order is misleading. It implies there is a beginning at Step 1 and an ending at Step 12. Recovery, however, like life, has a very ambiguous beginning and the ending clearly isn't always what we imagine it will be.

It might help to think of the steps as being arranged like a wheel rather than a ladder. Each time you move through a stage, you go into the hub, the center of your being, to check it out, see how it feels to you. Your actual process may begin at Step 5, then go to 2 and back to 6. Whether you engage in this process consciously or unconsciously, you are always seeing how something fits for you. Think of the process as helping you recognize where you are now and where you might move in the future as you continue your own

162

recovery. There are no accidents in life. If you are holding this book, there is something in it for you. Take from it what is useful for you at this time and leave the rest.

Although I will focus on love addiction I will touch on other related dependencies, since I have found that most clients have multiple addictions, with alcohol usually playing a key role.

These are the 12 steps I follow in treating people addicted to love:

(1) exploring the addictive process
(2) finding a guide
(3) understanding different types of addiction
(4) assessing risk
(5) evaluating the pros and cons of addiction
(6) trying the simple solution
(7) acknowledging where I am in the addictive process
(8) admitting the need for help
(9) deciding on a program
(10) developing safety, support, and abstinence
(11) dealing with grief, defenses, and the meaning of being an addict
(12) accepting a new life based on self-valuing and love

This program is different from most others in three significant ways. The first involves my belief that addiction isn't some aberration of the particularly deviant members of our society, but something that affects us all. We all feel there is something missing in our lives, that we are less than whole, and we all search for something to complete us. The nature of all addictions is the universal search to find something outside ourselves to help us feel secure, safe, and whole. The second involves my belief that we don't need to wait until a person bottoms out and admits their powerlessness before help can be given. I believe that for most people recovery begins much too late and only in response to extreme circumstances. If we are convinced that addiction is a very rare phenomenon that happens only to someone else—the poor, the homeless, the rich, the famous—it is easy to ignore the early warning signs and assume our unhappiness is caused by something else. The third involves my belief that there are actually positive aspects to addiction. Addicts need to accept the positive part addictions play in their lives before significant change can occur.

Let's take a more detailed look at the recovery process now, remembering that no one's recovery will proceed directly from Step 1 to 12:

STEP 1: EXPLORING THE ADDICTIVE PROCESS

Long before persons decide they have an addictive problem they begin to look at the ways they relate in the world. In the case of love addiction, people focus on their romantic relationships. They alternate between hope, as the possibility of a new relationship comes to the fore, and despair, when they go through the inevitable unhappy ending.

What we have learned about sex and romance is often quite distorted. As we grow up, popular movies and songs offer some strange notions about love. We hear that love is blind, to be truly in love is to suffer, that love is like a roller coaster that gives us the highs of ecstatic desire and the lows of devastating pain. We fall in love and become suddenly obsessed with *desire*.

We are conditioned to associate love with obsession not only through the popular media, but through our most profound literature. Shakespeare's *Romeo and Juliet* is a tragic tale of addiction. And Tolstoy's *Anna Karenina* has been acclaimed by some as the ultimate love story. It describes the relationship between the beautiful Anna and the dashing Count Vronsky. But listen to the way the consummation of their love is described: "That which for nearly a year had been the one absorbing desire of Vronsky's life, supplanting all his former desires; that which for Anna had been an impossible, terrible, but all the more bewitching dream of bliss, had come to pass." Are these feelings of love or the beginnings of addiction?

Dorothy Tennov, in her sensitive book *Love and Limerence: The Experience of Being in Love*, describes a process familiar to most of us: "You think, 'I want you. I want you forever, now, yesterday,

164

and always. Above all, I want you to want me. No matter where I am or what I am doing, I am not safe from your spell. At any moment, the image of your face smiling at me, of your voice telling me you care, or of your hand in mind, may suddenly fill my consciousness rudely pushing out all else.' "[1]

The first step in recovery—exploring the addictive process—may go on for years. It is a time of observing our behavior and it is usually done alone. Our insights often come in small flashes, small recognitions about our behavior, questions about what we are doing with our sexual and romantic lives. We often alternate between feeling that "something isn't right here" and blind faith that "things will be better tomorrow." We become increasingly confused.

We reach the end of Step 1 when we accept the fact that we're not sure whether or not we may have a problem, but that we need some guidance to help sort things out.

STEP 2: FINDING A GUIDE

It is crucial to find a guide if you want to recover from love addiction. Everyone who has an addiction also has a great fear of people. We are survivors and we have survived to this point, we believe, by being wary of people. We may have become superficially close but we've always kept our innermost selves protected. Now we have reached the point where we need to let someone in to that vulnerable inner self.

Many of us feel caught in a dilemma at this stage. We know that we can't continue to deal with our romantic behavior ourselves, yet we are afraid to allow anyone to get close enough to help us. When we hear about a "spiritual guide" we often react with indifference or anger. Either we can't relate to spiritual matters at all or the religion we knew as children is wrapped up with our abusive childhood, making it impossible to turn to it for comfort.

We are paralyzed by our tendency to think in absolute terms. Either I have *the* guide or I go it alone. Once I allow some other power to guide me, I will lose all my own power. If I pick a guide I don't like, I will be stuck with him or her for the rest of my life.

Let me suggest that learning to love again is a long process and that you will have many different guides along the way, each one just right for you. I recommend to people that they be open to guidance in many different forms. Be gentle with yourself. Choose a guide that is right for you *at this time*.

Guides I have used in my own recovery include:

- Books—I love to read and have had the experience of a book falling off the shelf, seemingly by accident. When I picked it up, I found it was just right for me.
- Music—Just the right song can often give me guidance in my search to understand my journey.
- A friend—Someone who just listened to me, cared without judging, and let me know I wasn't alone.
- A child—My own children, as well as other children, have often spoken to me about life and hope simply by their very presence in the world.
- My inner self—As a child I used to have imaginary friends I talked to constantly for support and comfort. As an adult I gave up childish things, knowing that my "friends" were just parts of me. Since I learned not to like or trust myself, I stopped talking and listening to myself. Yet there was always some part of me that was wise. When I began listening again I found I had a wonderful guide very close at hand.
- My higher power—This can be anything outside our own limited ego. It can be "God" as we understand him. It can be the "goddess" Nature, our recovery group, our own intuitive wisdom, or our psychotherapist. As with guides, we will often change our conception of higher power as our recovery progresses.
- A sponsor in one of the 12-step programs—Trusting another adult whom we do not know well is a huge step for many of us.[2] Yet being with someone who understands in their bones what we have been through because they have been through it themselves can provide great comfort.
- A professional counselor or therapist—A good counselor is someone who knows himself well, has wrestled with his own

166

addictions, has learned about sex and love addiction, and has his own program of recovery and spiritual development.

The best long-range guidance system I have found is a combination of your inner self, your higher power, and a "two-hatter."

A two-hatter is a person who is both an excellent psychotherapist or counselor and also a member of one of the 12-step programs, having recognized his or her own addiction and gotten help. Two-hatters are still relatively rare, but their number is growing. Look for them; it's worth the search.

If you can't find someone who actually wears both hats, look for someone who understands both. Seek out a psychotherapist who has attended at least one hundred 12-step meetings or look for a seasoned 12-step sponsor who has benefited from psychotherapy.

STEP 3: UNDERSTANDING DIFFERENT TYPES OF ADDICTION

I've found that there are many ways to begin the recovery process. Often we are blind to one addiction but can recognize that another aspect of our life is out of control. When we expand our definition of addictions—overeating, amassing money, gambling, dependence on tranquilizers—we have a better chance of finding the "hook" that will show us we need help. I've known many people who at first are blind to their love addiction, but recognize their cocaine use is getting out of hand. Others are able to recognize their problems with food long before they recognize their problems with people. Misunderstanding about the nature of addiction often delays our ability to find the way to recovery.

Since good food, money, sex, and power are so highly valued in our society, we are blind to the destruction they cause in the lives of so many. As we expand our understanding of all addictions, however, and recognize that if we are hooked on one thing we are likely to be hooked on others, we can become more sensitive to the range of addictions we may be engaged in and assess our personal risk factors.

167

STEP 4: ASSESSING RISK

One way to assess risk in the area of love addiction, as well as other addictions, is to do nothing and wait a few years to see how things go. If you have a romantic addiction it will get worse over time (though we will always look and find the times when things were good if we want to deny that we have a problem). Most people take this approach, aptly called the "ostrich" formula.

Another approach is to assume that any risk is too much risk. At the first sign of addictive problems some people ruthlessly attack the addiction on all fronts and refrain from any activity that is fun. This formula goes by the name of "the ultimate diet"—or the more masculine sounding "search-and-destroy."

The approach I prefer is one that neither allows us to do nothing, hoping against hope that things will improve, nor violates our being, or those we love, by trying to wipe out a part of ourselves. Rather it assumes that we are all addictive to a degree. Many of us can live with a low level of addictiveness. The time and energy it might take to change it is not worth the effort. For others, a low level may be too much. Such persons want to change.

I have found this reasonable approach very useful and this is why I dislike the typical questionnaires on addictions. After answering lots of questions that are obviously trying to prove we are alcoholic or something even more terrible, we get the feeling that if our score shows we "have it" we are doing a grave injustice to ourselves, our families, and the entire free world if we don't immediately check ourselves into a hospital.

The questionnaire at the end of the book is not designed to prove to you that you have a romantic addiction, but to help you define the degree of risk you face so you can decide for yourself what to do. The scores are determined by the experiences of many hundreds of people just like you who took the test so that they could see the place that love and romance had in their lives. Some who had low scores and minor problems decided they wanted to make changes anyway. Others had very high scores, but felt they weren't ready to change. When you are ready, take the test and use the information—along with what you've learned by reading this book—to help decide your own path.

STEP 5: EVALUATING THE PROS AND CONS OF ADDICTION

At first, most clients think it is ludicrous when I ask them to tell me all the positive things their addiction does for them. They are ready to have me take out my psychic scalpel and cut out the deadly addiction. They see their addiction as a cancer that is alien to them and that needs to be removed quickly and completely. Yet the more we talk and they begin to see how tightly they have held onto their addiction, treating it like a cherished lover or friend, they come to realize that their addiction means more to them than they originally had thought.

Kevin remembered breaking down in tears when he was first able to accept his addiction to alcohol as an old friend or lover. "I had turned to her in good times and in bad. She was there for me when no one else was. Even though things became destructive in the end, we had some wonderful times together. It was like thinking about an old lover. I knew we could never again be together, that we were destroying each other, but I still mourned the loss and cried for the love that never would be."

Unlike many who work in the field of addictions, I don't believe addictions should be given up immediately once they are recognized. As I pointed out earlier, I think there are both advantages and disadvantages to whatever addictions we have developed and there are advantages and disadvantages to giving them up.

Clients almost always express tremendous relief when I tell them they don't have to hate their addiction in order to move beyond it. In fact, hating it robs us of the ability to see it clearly and to learn what need the addiction served in our past. Rather than ripping it out heartlessly, we can replace it with something better over time so that the addiction just fades away. This is easier said than done, but it isn't as difficult as many people make it out to be.

I ask four questions of every person I work with who wishes to explore his or her love addiction:

169

(1) What are the specific problems you are having as a result of your love addiction?

(2) If you were not addicted to romance, how would your life be better?

(3) In what ways does your love addiction serve you?

(4) What are your fears about giving up your addiction?

Though the questions are simple, coming up with the answers is not easy, especially for questions 3 and 4.

I usually have people write their answers on four sheets of paper so that they can be put together and compared. One man's responses looked like this:

Disadvantages of romantic addiction:
　Keeps me tied up inside.
　I always feel scared.
　It keeps me from getting close to my wife.
　My preoccupation with beautiful women keeps me from being as effective at work as I once was.
　I feel guilty and ashamed.
Advantages of getting unhooked from romance:
　I would feel better about myself.
　My marriage would improve.
　I wouldn't feel so hyped and frantic all the time.
　I would feel calm.
　I could accomplish more at work if I didn't get distracted by pretty women.
　I think I would drink less if I didn't have the addiction in my life.
　I would feel sexier with my wife.
　I would like myself better.
　I would sleep better at night.
Positive things I get from my romantic addiction:
　I love the excitement of the hunt.
　I feel totally alive when I'm with a woman for the first time.
　My fantasies are like old friends. I love them.

170

My sexual activities are a reward for a lot of the shit I have to put up with in my life.

I don't have to think about my problems, I just have to plan my next romantic adventure.

It makes going to business meetings a lot more fun. There's always someone pretty I can watch.

They calm me down when I'm feeling too hyper and inflate me when I'm feeling depressed.

Negative things about stopping my romantic addiction:

I'm afraid I couldn't do it.

I'd feel like a total failure if I couldn't stop.

Sex would be dull and boring.

I'd have to look inside me and I don't like what I think I'd find.

I don't know what I'd do with my time.

I'd be alone in the world, like an orphan.

I'd have to look at some things in our marriage that I'd rather not have to look at.

When we weigh all these factors we get a clearer picture of our options. When we deny that there are any advantages to our addiction and that we have no negative feelings about stopping, we continue to believe we want to stop while our actions indicate the opposite. Only by looking honestly at all our answers can we begin to deal effectively with our romantic addiction.

STEP 6: TRYING THE SIMPLE SOLUTION

Everyone who has a romantic addiction wants to try the simple solution first. No one wants to make major life changes. When we do conclude that we need to change our behavior, we search for the change that will be the least disruptive to our old patterns. If we have a drinking problem, we'd prefer just to change our brand of booze, or switch from whiskey to beer or from vodka to wine. We decide to drink only on weekends or never before five o'clock.

As love addicts, we often pick one aspect of our addiction and try to convince ourselves that by eliminating that one thing everything will be okay—we won't have to make any big changes. We may break off an affair with a particular person or stop flirting in the office. We may decide that all we need is more fun in our lives and take a cruise with our wife. It obviously doesn't make all our problems go away, but sometimes we are at a point in our lives where one change can tip the balance. We still must make other changes to keep ourselves healthy and reverse the addictive ways in which we have been living. But sometimes small changes can work wonders. Don't discount them.

On the other hand, we need to guard against deluding ourselves with many different "simple solutions"—trying one after the next while our addiction continues to get worse. If the simple solution doesn't work, it is time to take a serious look at the addictive process and how it is affecting our lives. This is one of the major advantages of having a guide to work with.

STEP 7: ACKNOWLEDGING WHERE I AM IN THE ADDICTIVE PROCESS

It's part of human nature to avoid what we are afraid of. Many people are afraid that they might have a cavity and so avoid the dentist. We avoid doctors and checkups because we are afraid we have cancer. Everyone is afraid their kids might become hooked on drugs; we therefore avoid talking about drug use.

Romantic activities touch the most basic needs we have. It will never be easy to look honestly at ourselves in this context. I would go so far as to say that alone no one can honestly see where he or she is in the addictive process. The best we can do is to put ourselves in the way of others who have the courage to be honest and tell us what they see. This is why a guide is absolutely essential. Only someone close to us can see the behaviors that we ourselves will deny. Even with guidance it may be a long time before we can say: "This is where I am."

If you can say that, you are ready to accept the truth. You have taken a serious look at your addictive behavior. You have tried the simple solution, possibly a number of them.

172

The questionnaire at the end of this book may take on new meaning now. If you've taken the test before, take it again. Ask your guide or others close to you how they perceive you in relation to the questions. But remember: No matter what others tell you about your situation, whether they feel you are having minor problems with your romantic addictions, whether they feel the problems are serious, or even immediately life-threatening, you must be the final judge.

STEP 8: ADMITTING THE NEED FOR HELP

You acknowledged the possibility that you might need help when you first picked up this book. Somewhere deep inside there was a voice that said: "My life isn't right. Something is wrong somewhere." As you've gotten closer to this step, there has been a heightened awareness of your situation. The closer you've come to it the more terrified you've become. It has become clear to you that if you continue along your current path death and destruction await you. And admitting you need help is also terrifying.

You took one big step when you began the process of dealing with your addiction, another when you took the risk to reach out to a guide. But you also know that your involvement in the process up until now hasn't been totally serious. You still have the feeling that "I'm just checking this out. I can stop any time I want."

Now you are at a crucial crossroad, perhaps the most crucial one in your life. Make the wrong choice and your life is likely to continue to cause you pain and lead you onward to destruction. Make the right choice and your life will begin to be filled with peace and happiness.

You are aware that the old way doesn't work. But it's familiar and familiarity counts for a lot in your life. Admitting you have a problem requires an act of total surrender. Some describe it as "being sick and tired of being sick and tired."

At decisive points in your life you've usually gone with what you know. Yet now you've begun taking risks and are finding that there is a new way to be, that you can change for the better. There is a

173

small voice inside that says "Maybe, just maybe, surrendering and admitting that I have a problem might help me."

Ultimately it's like jumping off into the unknown. When you finally make the jump, you won't know whether you jumped or someone pushed you. As you move up to that point the terror will increase. As you jump you will feel suspended between life and death.

But the moment you take that leap and say "Yes, I do have a problem. My love life is out of control. I can't do it myself. Please help me!" you will be free.

No one can really tell you what it is like on the other side of surrender. You have to experience it to know it. When you are ready you will experience it. When you do, you will feel a weight has lifted and you will be ready for the next step in your recovery.

STEP 9: DECIDING ON A PROGRAM

There are three types of programs to choose from, depending on your needs and the resources available to you. The first is a residential program, in which you live away from home for a period of time. This is an extreme solution for most people. Its advantage is that you are able to separate yourself from the pressures of your day-to-day life and focus fully on your romantic addiction. You don't have to worry about preparing meals or going off to work. Most addicts are sure they don't have time to devote to a residential program, though they usually find time for a vacation and have *always* had time to indulge their addiction.

The second type of program is a nonresidential or outpatient program. You meet regularly with a trained counselor who specializes in treating romantic addiction. You may be part of a group in which you would be able to interact with others who are also sexually and romantically addicted. The advantage of this type of program is that you can remain at home and continue on your job for the duration of treatment.

Any good residential or outpatient program will involve the family in the treatment program, since all recognize the necessity of

174

family participation if recovery is to be successful. Most also involve the person and the family in one of the 12-step programs that focus on romantic addiction.

The third type of program offers total involvement in a 12-step program such as Sex and Love Addicts Anonymous, Sexaholics Anonymous, or Sex Addicts Anonymous. There has often been a professional bias against these mutual-support, self-help groups. Some professionals believe that if you aren't certified and licensed to practice therapy you won't be of maximum help to others needing help. But the success of these programs is proof that these programs can be effective without professional leadership.

My own experience is that the best course for most individuals combines both professional and self-help approaches. Some people begin by seeing a professional and later get involved in a self-help group. Others begin in a group and find later that they benefit from additional help from a professional.

STEP 10: DEVELOPING SAFETY, SUPPORT, AND ABSTINENCE

Our addictions were our security blankets. They were the only thing we knew we could trust. But we came to know that what had once given us comfort was now hurting us. We knew we had to give it up, yet were determined to hold on to our blanket until we were ready. Readiness was always a bit different for each of us. But in all cases the key element that allowed us to make the leap of faith was the feeling of total safety and security.

Whether we initially choose a 12-step program or a professional counselor, we need to feel absolutely safe. Our first priority is to ensure our physical safety. Those of us who are romance addicts need to know that the people we entrust ourselves to can be relied on not to touch us sexually or "hit" on us in any way.

The second priority is to be emotionally accepted for who we are. We need to be able to tell our story to people who will understand us and not judge us.

It's important that we choose our people well. But having chosen them, we need to allow them to be human. Only in our fantasy

175

world are people all-loving, all-nurturing. In the real world we know that absolute safety and security are an illusion. No matter how fine our therapist or how supportive our sponsor, they too will make mistakes and may even do things to threaten our trust in them. I've known many people who dropped their program at this stage because of such disappointments. They discover people in the self-help groups who still act out their love addiction, just as alcoholics find people in AA who fall off the wagon. They realize their therapist isn't as all-loving as they thought.

The key to developing safety and security is to find a support network made up of a number of good people so that when one falters, as all humans will, there are other resources. This is why 12-step programs all stress the principles rather than individual personalities. The more we rely on principle and accept that humans will never follow principle perfectly, the faster we can move ahead with our recovery.

Along with offering safety and security, our recovery program will teach us to define abstinence. We begin to live our lives with abstinence at the core of our program.

Many of us wish that abstinence would be defined absolutely. At this stage of our recovery, we value the security we feel from absolutes. We don't like having to make too many choices. We may wish we were "just" alcoholic or drug-addicted so the meaning of abstinence would be simple—give up alcohol or heroin.

Love addicts must learn to define what behaviors they must give up in order to begin their recovery. For some abstinence must be defined very narrowly: "I had to give up all sexual activity except having intercourse with my wife." Another person may have another bottom line: "I have to stop reading so many romance novels and deal with my husband and his reality. I have to live in the real world with real emotions and allow myself to connect with my husband."

At this stage know that you have a support system and that whatever decisions you make about abstinence can be modified as experience dictates. "I found I had to add more things to my list of behaviors I needed to cut out," Kevin says. "At first I thought

I could handle looking at magazines. I thought that as long as I wasn't getting involved with clients it was enough. But I found that the fantasies I played with while looking at the magazines always led to fantasies about my clients. The magazines weren't dangerous in themselves but they led me back into dangerous territory. I had to give them up too."

Often our fear is that if we give up a behavior that has meant so much to us we will become even more obsessed and "crazy." We reason that if we could just "do it a little bit," it would take the edge off. But the reality for most is that when we get clear about those activities we must abstain from, and stick with that knowledge absolutely, our preoccupation lessens. We find that we are able to live quite well without them.

This whole process may take some time and a strong program with good support will enable you to move to the next step.

STEP 11: DEALING WITH GRIEF, DEFENSES, AND THE MEANING OF BEING AN ADDICT

When we assessed all the pros and cons of our addiction we realized that there were many aspects of our romantic lives that we valued. They were like old friends and lovers.

Initially, when we began our recovery program, we were glad to get rid of these old but "bad" friends. Now we may feel the loss, as if some part of us had died. We need to grieve. In order to move ahead with our recovery we must actually go through the same mourning process as if a loved one had died.

At first we can't believe we have lost this old friend. "Someday I'll be able to do that again." Then we go through an angry time. We are mad at everyone—our therapist, our spouse, our friends. We're mad at them for taking away our goodies. We're even mad at our addictions. Later we go through a time of bargaining. "If I stopped seeing my lover for a year, then I'd be able to go back, right?" We hope against hope that there is some way we can have our cake and eat it too.

When it's clear the loss is final, we become very depressed. We

177

may cry about our lost past. We feel alone again and all the support we have seems useless. It's the acceptance of loss, though, that eventually leads us back to ourselves. We know our old life is finished and so we are able to move on.

Along with accepting the loss of our addiction, we come to see that many of the defenses we used in order to survive the past are interfering now with our continued recovery.

Many of us tended to blame others for our misfortunes. It seemed the only way we could keep from killing ourselves was always to see ourselves as blameless and others as causing our problems. Now we begin to see that our harsh judgment and blaming of others was a defense we used against taking responsibility for ourselves and against letting others get close to us. Alternatively, some of us took the opposite tack to survive: We assumed if there was a problem, it must be our fault. Now we begin to see that we needed to assert our own strength and tell others when we thought they were at fault. Whatever defenses we employed earlier, we begin to examine them and modify them in light of our newfound strength.

The final task of this stage is to come to terms with what it means for us to be an addict. For most of us our early beliefs about addiction merged with our early beliefs about ourselves. We believed we were born bad and unworthy and that nothing we did could make us good and valuable, but we had to keep trying.

At this point we come to see that to be an addict is to be human. To accept our addiction and develop a program of recovery for ourselves can take us beyond just being "normal"—it can help us lead a life of real value. Being an addict means that we must continue on a path that brings peace and love to ourselves and others. When we glimpse this reality we are ready for the last step in the recovery process.

STEP 12: ACCEPTING A NEW LIFE BASED ON SELF-VALUING AND LOVE

In many ways our journey ends where it began. We came into the world perfect, loving creatures as valuable and loved as anything in the universe. Like all human creatures we forgot we were perfect. We thought there was something "out there" that would replace what we thought was missing in us. Our romantic addiction took us on a journey to find the love we thought we had lost. Having looked in all the wrong places, we have come to see that the place we were afraid to look was inside ourselves.

At this stage our conception of a "higher power" and our idea of "a power within" merge. We see that the God we searched for, raged at, and rejected is really in us. We are all God. We come to see that the love we sought, but were always afraid to receive, was in us all the time. We come to see that the world is full of supportive people who love and accept us. We needed only to love and accept ourselves to see that. We have learned too that all people are on a journey of love, and when people seem to hurt us or reject us, it is only because of their own fear and pain.

Just as we learn we are not victims but survivors, we learn too that we are not targets of others' malice, but fellow travelers on a journey toward love.

At this stage we can forgive our parents for the wrongs we are sure they caused us. We can see that they too were damaged as children and passed on to us the hurts and fears that they carried. We come to accept that our parents did the best they could. And we come to see that they gave us the greatest gift there is.

They gave us life.

Finally, we see that in fact the gift of life is all we ever needed. We accept that our journey has been wondrous. All the pain of looking for love in all the wrong places, all the fear and anger has brought us to the love we had been searching for. We recognize and accept this love precisely because we have journeyed. We haven't gotten to where we are in spite of our past, but because of it.

Remember the leaf experience I learned as a child? Each one of the dots on the outside of the leaf represents one of the experiences of "looking for love in the wrong place." Each stroke on the inside helped me see where love could truly be found. I needed the entire experience. I needed to look for love in all the wrong places to truly accept the real places when I found them.

One of the gifts of life is that the journey never ends. We can never have too much love and we can never stop learning how to love better.

In the next chapter we will explore in depth the meaning of healthy attitudes toward sexuality, romance, and love in a world that seems to have lost its way.

9. HEALTHY LOVE:
Illusion or Reality?

Giving Up Romance to Find Love

The only permanent cure for love addiction is to find a new level of love and intimacy. As romance addicts, we have never experienced real love. We didn't learn it from our parents. We were surrounded from birth by messages that told us that the world was unsafe, that it was impossible to get what we wanted, but that we must keep searching.

Society also gave us confusing messages about sex. We were led to believe that the sexual revolution freed us from fear and unnecessary constraint. Instead it took us from seeing sexual freedom first as a goal we should all seek, to an expectation we must all meet, then to a standard that no one could live up to, and finally to a societal obsession that few could resist.

George Leonard has observed the danger in society's misunderstanding of sex and erotic love.[1] He sees our modern preoccupation with sexual freedom as a mirror image of the Victorian repression of sexual pleasure.

The positive side of our addiction was that we never gave up trying to find the love we knew was ours, but that we never received

181

as children. We spent our lives trying to find the security we never had, looking to wrap ourselves up in the arms of a perfect mother, a perfect father, a perfect lover.

Some of us turned to professional educators and therapists who were supposed to help us overcome our sexual hang-ups, learn to communicate our romantic needs, and enjoy "healthy love practices." We often did learn to overcome sexual dysfunction, but this didn't help to overcome our romantic addiction.

Addiction recovery programs helped. But few of us would be satisfied for long in just getting rid of our love addiction.

At the beginning of our recovery, many of us felt that anything would be better than the life we were leading. But once our recovery progressed, we found we still hungered for a healthy and happy relationship filled with security, love, intimacy, and comfort, a relationship that contributed to our feeling of worth and value.

We found that learning to love had little to do with learning the right lovemaking techniques, but rather with recognizing and overcoming past fears, getting comfortable with ourselves, seeking a partner to grow with us rather than one who would complete us.

We found that most of what we learned about love was really about how to survive and feel secure. Learning to love means letting go of our old patterns and ways of looking at the world and being willing to start anew.

We found the love we were looking for by giving up our search for romance.

To most of us that statement sounded like a death sentence at first. Romance had been the lifeblood that flowed through our veins. To give up the search for romance was like watching ourselves bleed to death slowly. Yet through our recovery program we found that we did not die without the kind of romantic relationships we once had.

Looking back at the active addiction phase of our lives, we see that many of the things we did to make our lives better actually made them worse. The men and women we fell madly in love with turned out to be bad for us. The compulsive romantic behaviors we felt we needed in order to make us feel high actually caused us to feel even more depressed. We often felt we were operating with a faulty compass that always pointed south instead of north. Rather than question our homing device, we questioned ourselves or our partners. We were convinced that either we were "doing it wrong" and just needed to try harder to "get it right" or our partner was the problem and we just needed to find the right partner.

Many of us began our recovery by doing what *didn't* feel good, trusting that if we went in the opposite direction from the one we felt drawn to, we'd be better off than following the old pattern. One man in recovery put it this way: "I began to distrust the type of woman I was attracted to. When I would get that rush of excitement, that feeling of being drawn almost out of my skin, I knew I had to run the other way. I knew that a woman who stimulated that kind of feeling in me would destroy me. It took a long while to be willing to move away from the very experiences I had always been drawn to, but it worked. It took that kind of determination to stay unhooked long enough to find out what kind of person I really wanted to be with."

When I suggested that we must be willing to give up the search for romance I didn't mean that we must be celibate the rest of our lives and live on a cold mountaintop without any excitement or love. Rather it is the compulsive search for sexual thrills that we must give up. As long as we are on the lookout for "romance" we're telling ourselves we "need" it to survive. We're also telling ourselves that there's something called "romance" that's separate from human interaction. But we've seen that to pursue that path does *not* get us what we want. We've learned from experience that though the pull is strong, almost magnetic, it doesn't draw us toward love. We've finally recognized that it just led to another "wrong place."

The Right Place for Love

We've been trying to find love without taking any risks. One of the first lessons we learned in childhood, after all, was that we can't trust people. The result was that we searched for fantasy love to avoid getting hurt.

It's as though our inner guidance system has been saying to us:

183

"Look, you know you can't trust anybody. You've been burned too many times to take another risk. Remember what happened with your mother and don't forget your father. Brothers and sisters, uncles and aunts—no one you know intimately can be trusted. You've got to have romance in order to survive. The best way to get it is by distilling it out of the human situation. Go after the romance, but don't get close to the people. You may need to wear a number of masks to do it, because you can't let anyone know who you really are, what you really feel, or you'll get hurt again. Don't get emotionally involved. Your survival depends upon it."

The process of recovery has allowed us to gain the inner strength to give up our addictive patterns of conquest and romantic intrigue so that we can allow something else to come in.[2]

There is an old story of a learned man going to visit a Zen Buddhist monk. The man had heard that the monk could teach him things about life that would enable him to be happy. The man made his way to the small hut in the mountains where the monk lived, and the monk invited him in. The man started talking as soon as he entered the hut. He described his background, told the monk about the various degrees he had earned from prestigious universities, and almost demanded that the monk teach him about the mysteries of life. The monk smiled gently and asked the man to sit down and have some tea. After preparing the tea with great care, the monk brought the pot to the small table where the man sat. The man offered his cup to the monk, who poured the tea— and kept pouring the tea. It overflowed the sides and spilled all over the man's expensive designer suit. The man jumped up sputtering, "What's the matter with you? Can't you see that my cup is already full?" "Yes," said the monk, "I can see that it is. And I have nothing I can teach you until you first empty your cup."

In order to find the "right" places to find love, we must be willing to stop looking in the "wrong" places. We must be willing to stop looking for an addictive partner, whether the perfect romantic partner or a partner for physical excitement. When we give up the search and recognize that we won't die as a consequence, we are ready to find the "right" place to look for love.

In order to do this we must recognize how dependent we've

184

become on finding the magical "other" we hope will complete us. As long as we deny our dependency—or our strength—our search for the "other" dominates our lives.

My Own Search For Love

As a light at the end of the tunnel, I offer my own personal experience of finding healthy love. Over the years, I often helped myself get clear about some important issue in my life by teaching a class on it. Someone said that we always teach what we want to learn.

My class "Men's Liberation/Women's Liberation: If It's So Good, Why Aren't We Happy?" helped me acknowledge my own dependency on women. We discussed the reasons people cling to old beliefs about the psychological differences between men and women in spite of the changes of the past twenty years. Men are "destined" to be active in the world, to dominate, make things happen. Women are destined to remain at home to take care of the house, the children, and their husbands.

Many men and women are frustrated that "liberation" hasn't occurred more rapidly. Some blame themselves, others blame their partner. Many blame the opposite sex as a whole. A recent cover story in *Time* magazine (1987) headlined: "Are Women Fed Up?— A hotly disputed Hite Report says yes—and that men are to blame."

It is understandable, though somewhat naive, to hope that beliefs about the role of men and women, sex and romance, love and life that go back thousands of years should change in ten or twenty years. For we have failed to recognize the power of myths, basic beliefs about the way the world is supposed to operate that have guided human beings throughout history. Our rational thought tells us that men and women must be treated equally, but myths operate on another level of reality. They speak to our deepest longings, fears, expectations, and dreams. Until we understand the power of myths we will continue to feel angry and frustrated that our love relationships don't improve.

One of these cherished basic beliefs is the myth of female weakness, that women are fragile and need to be protected by men. We

185

may wish this belief would go away, but it is a powerful force for both men and women. Men still believe that they must support both themselves and a woman, and women still dream about a man who will sweep them off their feet and provide for their needs.

Yet when we explore this myth, we recognize that beneath it is another myth: the belief in the power of women. Both men and women are born of a woman who is all-powerful and on whom we are dependent for our very existence. Many believe that men's desire to keep women under their thumb is because men secretly fear women's power. Keeping these myths out of our consciousness presents an interesting dilemma for men and women who fall in love.

A man grows up to marry a woman who he is "supposed" to dominate, but who he is deeply dependent upon and frightened of being hurt by. A woman marries a man she is "supposed" to be subservient to, but who she deeply resents and feels superior to.

I shared with the class my feeling that the first step of my own liberation was to recognize and acknowledge my own fears and dependency on women. It was only then that I could begin to assert my real strength and let go of my compulsive need to dominate these creatures I secretly feared and needed.

I told the class about a group experience I had recently had in which we did a "fishbowl" exercise. The women sat in a circle in the middle of the floor and were the first to talk about their experiences while the men listened. I felt envious at the ease with which the women shared their feelings with each other and the way they opened up with real concerns and fears.

When the women finished and we men began to move into the circle, one woman patted the place she had just vacated as if to say, "Here, take my place and be comfortable." I nodded a thanks, sat down, then immediately moved as if I had sat down on a hot griddle. She patted the spot again and I moved back to sit where she indicated. Once again I jumped, chose another spot, and this time burst into tears. This had all occurred in a period of twenty seconds as the men's group was forming.

Through my tears I finally was able to say what I was feeling. The invitation to "sit here" was one I had responded to all my life.

186

I knew that women had some magic "power" that I could perhaps grasp if I got very close to them. My whole history of romantic addiction was related to this long-buried need.

It was as though I had always had a cord attached to me that I needed to plug into a woman in order to get the power to live. In that moment of moving into the circle I knew I had been following that pattern all my life and that I couldn't do it anymore. I had to find my own place, my own source of power. My tears were for the joy of finally seeking my own power and for the fear that I would die without getting it from a woman.

Most of the men could identify with my feeling of seeking some kind of power from women. It was a power we associated with producing life, being loving, and caring about children and the world. We all felt we lacked, or had lost, some sense of that power and beauty. We felt we were playing out the story of Beauty and the Beast and could only find our salvation by having a beautiful woman see through our ugliness and love us.

As the men talked we began to understand the ways in which romantic addiction was a natural response to that deeply held belief. There was a moment of quiet when we each woke up to the fact that what had been lost could never be found by looking to women. If it were to be found at all, it would be by looking within. Of course, the parallel is true for women: The lost part can't be found in a male partner, but only in herself.

It took me many more months to get another glimpse of where to look for love. I was tired of affairs, tired of looking for the "perfect" wife, tired of sex altogether. In a moment of despair I cried, "Where is the great love of my life?" As I lay on my bed with my eyes closed I began to see pictures in my mind of all the loves of my life—all the women I had reached out for, each time hoping that I would find my savior. As I pictured each one I began to cry as they each, in turn, receded into darkness.

I kept going back in time. I saw my second wife before my eyes, then my first wife, and many lovers in between. I finally went back to my first girlfriend, when I was eight years old. The farther back I went the deeper I sobbed. Finally, I got back to my mother and I cried for the little boy who didn't get the love he should have had. It seemed that I had lost everything, and I cried with utter despair.

When I thought there were no more tears, I felt the floor of my being open up. I fell through it, and came face to face with the great love of my life. She was the woman in me. She was a kind of female reflection of my inner essence. I gasped with the recognition that this was who I had been looking for all my life. And in that moment I began to cry again, for all the times I had betrayed her. I thought of all the women I had lusted over, looking for the perfect body, the perfect partner. I poured out my guilt at having left my only true love.

But the tears turned from tears of shame to tears of gratitude as I realized that this "woman" had never left me. She was quietly waiting for me to wake up and recognize that the object of my search was within.

In the months following that experience, I felt peaceful for the first time in my life. I knew that I didn't need a woman in order to survive. I knew that no woman out in the world could ever make me happy or fill the void I felt inside. I felt loved as I never had before. I felt complete.

I noticed the change in many small ways. For the first time I could come home after work and not immediately turn on the TV to hear a human voice. When faced with the choice of going out looking for action and having a quiet evening with myself, I chose to stay alone and found I actually enjoyed my own company. I didn't have to keep busy all the time. I found I could go for quiet walks without any destination or purpose. In short, I didn't feel driven.

I thought that maybe this was the end of the journey, that I was to learn that I didn't need a woman and would spend the rest of my life as a contented monk. That's not how it ended, however.

I met the woman I've been with now for over eight years. We have shared more joy and happiness than I ever thought possible. I'd like to share a little of our experience together and contrast this kind of love with the addictive love I had experienced for most of my life.

I must say that we're still learning about love and what it means to people recovering from romantic addiction. Please take these thoughts as preliminary findings of a couple newly embarked on the journey, not as the last word.

This Couldn't Be Love . . .

We met at the kind of retreat I had always loved to attend, where the stated focus was "expanding human potential" but the underlying agenda for me was always finding that certain someone or a warm sexual partner. In the past my first order of business was to check out the women to see who I would approach later. This time I became immersed helping in the kitchen, a job I had always shunned because it was so invisible.

The retreat was to last a week, and two days passed before I made contact with a woman. This was highly unusual for me. The longest I had ever waited for making my move on someone was about six minutes. Here I was in a beautiful beach-front setting with two hundred "enlightened" people, half of them available women—and I was just enjoying the people, the surf, and my own company.

When Carlin approached me, she made it clear she was interested in me and wondered why I had been avoiding her. The encounter was unusual in a number of respects. The first was that I was approached by a woman at all. This had never happened to me before. I never waited to see who might be interested in me (secretly I feared that no one would be), but always made the first move. I learned the agonies of being rejected by someone I was attracted to, and the excitement of winning a prize beauty I had been stalking for hours.

Second, I was surprised that I hadn't picked up Carlin's interest in me sooner. Part of the meeting/mating ritual for me had always depended upon my keen sense of who was giving me "the eye." A woman rarely made the first move overtly, but usually sent out little looks and vibes that told me she was available. Picking up on these subtle clues was essential to minimize the possibility of being rejected (which always hurt deeply, even after I'd been through it a thousand times).

189

Third, I realized that Carlin wasn't really my "type." She *was* attractive, and in the past that was all that was necessary for me to express an interest. Yet the women who really turned me on often had a certain look to them. They were short, shorter than me at 5 feet 5 inches—I just couldn't feel like a man if a woman was even a hair taller than I. They usually had dark hair, a trim sexy body, and an outgoing personality. Carlin was taller than I was, had light brown hair, and though sexy and outgoing, she had a quiet reserve about her. She definitely didn't fit my fantasy-lover image.

As the attraction deepened and I began to feel more interested in her, there were even more changes to deal with. The thing that struck me as we spent more time together during the week was how much fun we were having and how easy things were. There was a difference between Carlin and other women I had been attracted to in the way we related to one another. With other women there was always a certain kind of tension that seemed to heighten the passion and excitement, the "chemistry" between us. With Carlin there was no tension. She felt more like an old friend I'd known for years than a new lover.

In the past there had always been elements of a contest involved in meeting a new woman. If I was interested I would always make the first approach and assume that I had to impress her in some way to draw her to me. I prided myself on not coming on with a phony line and in fact saw myself as very honest in meeting new women. Yet there was still a strong element of "putting my best foot forward" and emphasizing those qualities I supposed she'd want in a man.

With Carlin I felt none of that. I told myself it was because I wasn't really interested in getting involved. I was enjoying my freedom and though I wasn't opposed to spending time together, I was beginning to feel my sense of self more strongly and wasn't hooked on "falling in love" any longer.

An interesting term, "falling in love." It has the quality of an act that happens to us, rather than something we choose. There is a feeling of losing control, giving ourselves over to another person or to the passion of the moment. Earlier, when I would meet a

190

woman for the first time to whom I was very attracted, I would always have the feeling of "falling." Sometimes it felt like "falling in love," at other times it was clearly a matter of "falling in lust."

I pictured myself sometimes gently rowing a canoe across a lake on a beautiful summer day. I'd be relaxed and comfortable, alone and enjoying my own company. Suddenly the current would begin to increase and I'd begin to move faster. I realized that somehow I was now in a river being drawn by a powerful current. My focus had narrowed to watching what was immediately in front of me. As the current speeded up even more I felt a mixture of excitement and fear as it became evident that I couldn't affect the path of the boat and must give myself over to the force. It felt wonderful. As I was drawn down the river there would be no time to be bored or to deal with life's little problems. I'd feel free of the past and ready to plunge on into the future. I didn't know what was ahead, maybe calm waters or a dangerous waterfall. I didn't care. The rush and excitement was too great.

That's how it would often feel to me to fall in love. I would feel that "it" had come out of the blue. I was struck by lightning and my life changed instantly. My attention narrowed—as the song said, "I only have eyes for you." When I got the same adoring stare back, I felt I'd entered an altered state. I was lost in love.

When I met Carlin I didn't feel any of these things. Instead of the passionate rush of someone being drawn down a raging stream, I continued to feel the calm of rowing myself across a beautiful lake. The difference was that now I had another person to share it with, a partner. In my earlier relationships I felt caught in a cyclone, sucked up in the air and taken on a wild ride. With Carlin it was like being in the center of the cyclone, still high above the earth, but in the calm center of things. I could still see the swirling energy being pulled around the outside, but in the center we could laugh and play like children.

It was wonderful. I'd never felt anything like it in my life. For the first time I was with a woman I felt totally relaxed and comfortable with. I felt I had finally come home. We spent another week together and made plans to see each other more. I was ecstatic. I did what any all-American boy (read addict) would do.

I concluded that this couldn't be love and proceeded to search out the first woman I could find to have an affair with.

My reasoning seemed logical at the time. I *knew* what love was like. There was uncontrolled passion, bells and whistles would go off when you touched, and you would scream with delight when you made love. You knew you had found that certain someone and had to damn well make sure you kept her and that none of the other wolves prowling around could get close to her.

The fact that all these other "love" relationships had quickly turned to disappointment, fear, anger, blame, and disillusionment only fueled my desire to find someone different and try again. I never noticed that all the "different" women I chose had a basic similarity about them that began the same destructive cycle all over again.

The only thing that saved me from repeating my old patterns was that Carlin was not as addictive as I was. She made it quite clear that I'd have to choose between her and "other women," and I'd have to make the choice immediately. She wasn't interested in hanging around while I sorted things out. The other factor that kept me from wrecking this new relationship was a tiny voice that whispered inside my head that maybe my old perception of love wasn't quite right.

I certainly could not deny the passion, excitement, danger, and desire I felt for the women I had previously fallen in love with. But I also couldn't deny that there was pain, broken promises, and disappointment. If that was love, I thought, maybe I'd try monkish boredom. But what I was now finding with Carlin wasn't boring at all. It was a different kind of excitement, one that I'd never experienced.

I came to see that the "rush" I had always associated with falling in love was really not love at all. It was the addictive excitement that a drowning person feels when he thinks he's found a life preserver. The excitement, passion, danger, and desire are surely there. But the feelings have more to do with survival, safety, and security than they do with friendship, self-esteem, and love.

When I recognized that I was beginning to love for the first time in my life, I slowly let go of each one of my beliefs about romance.

192

At first I thought I was letting go of passion. Our love seemed so quiet and easy. It didn't seem to have the "edge" that I was used to from the past. I didn't lose all my other interests as I usually did when I fell in love. I continued to see other friends and remained involved with my work.

I came to see that there is a whole new kind of passion that is created when two people come together who don't need each other, but very much want each other. It is a passion that derives its energy from the spirit. It comes when we realize that we are already complete human beings. We don't need another person in order to complete us. We give because we feel so full of love it overflows onto another person, not because the other person has something we desperately need. "I love you" means "I'm so full of love I want to share it with you." It doesn't mean "I'm so unworthy alone that only in your presence do I feel validated."

Carlin and I are still discovering what it means to love and how this new kind of love differs from addictive love. Growing up in families that were addictive, in a society that is addictive, we had difficulty in developing a clear picture of the difference. What follows is a summary of what we've learned so far.

Healthy Love and Addictive Love

All of us have a healthy impulse to find love, but our addictions take us away from genuine love. I believe a summary of the differences between Healthy Love and Addictive Love can help us find the genuine love we all seek and deserve.

1. Healthy Love develops after we feel secure.
   Addictive Love tries to create love even though we feel frightened and insecure.
2. Healthy Love comes from feeling full. We overflow with love.
   Addictive Love is always trying to fill an inner void.
3. Healthy Love begins with loving ourselves, being the lover we feel we need.
   Addictive Love keeps us from looking at ourselves honestly and always seeks to get love from that "special someone."

193

4. Healthy Love comes to us once we've given up the search.
   Addictive Love is always sought after.
5. Healthy Love is part of the human fabric. It can't be separated from it.
   Addictive Love is highly distilled. We think we can separate "it" from people, whether the "it" is sex or romantic intrigue.
6. Healthy Love allows us to be vulnerable because we feel secure inside.
   Addictive Love is based on a shaky foundation. We feel we must always protect ourselves.
7. Healthy Love grows slowly, like a tree.
   Addictive Love grows fast, as if by magic, like those children's animals that expand instantly when we add water.
8. Healthy Love thrives on time alone as well as time with our partner.
   Addictive Love is frightened of being alone.
9. Healthy Love is derived from a balance of masculine and feminine qualities within each person.
   Addictive Love creates super-masculine and super-feminine qualities and encourages us to search for our "missing half" in another person.
10. Healthy Love encourages us to feel we have the power to create our own world and be happy.
    Addictive Love sees others as having power over us. We seek the "perfect" partner because of the power that person seems to bring us.
11. Healthy Love is unique. There is no "ideal" lover I seek.
    Addictive Love is stereotyped. There is always a certain type we are attracted to.
12. Healthy Love is gentle and comfortable.
    Addictive Love is tense and combative.
13. Healthy Love encourages us to be ourselves, to be honest from the beginning with who we are, including our faults.
    Addictive Love encourages secrets. We always want to look good and put on an attractive mask.

14. Healthy Love creates a deeper sense of ourselves the longer we are together.

    Addictive Love creates a loss of self the longer we are together.
15. Healthy Love gets easier as time goes on.

    Addictive Love requires more effort as time goes on. It's hard to sustain a romantic image.
16. Healthy Love develops as fear decreases.

    Addictive Love expands as fear increases.
17. Healthy Love is satisfied with the partner we have.

    Addictive Love is always looking for "more" or "better."
18. Healthy Love encourages us to broaden our interests.

    Addictive Love encourages us to narrow our interests.
19. Healthy Love is based on the belief that we want to be together.

    Addictive Love is based on the belief that we have to be together.
20. Healthy Love teaches that we can only make ourselves happy.

    Addictive Love expects the other person to make us happy and demands that we try to make them happy.
21. Healthy Love creates life.

    Addictive Love creates melodramas.

Carlin and I have found that the process of love is as important as the content. The core of the process for us has been a willingness to make a commitment to ourselves and the relationship. To love her, I need to love myself; and to truly love myself I have to be willing to extend my love to Carlin. We find that this kind of love requires active attention.

We both plan times to be alone, to recharge our own batteries and focus on ourselves. We also plan time together. Wednesday is our special night and we make it a high enough priority in our lives that our work, children, friends, and family rarely interfere with our evening together.

Paradoxically, being committed to Carlin doesn't mean I believe there is no one else in the world who I could be happy with. The belief that there is only one person who can make us happy is dangerous. Rather than adding to our security, it actually fuels our fear. We become frantic to find the right person and hold on to them for dear life. This fear kills many relationships.

Carlin and I know we are together out of choice. We could be happy with someone else, but we choose to be with each other. This feeling of choice extends into our day-to-day world. Although in times of stress I'm convinced that there are some things that I absolutely "need" from Carlin, I remind myself that though I might "prefer" her to touch me, for instance, I will survive without it. This recognition keeps us from making immature and overbearing demands on each other.

It's been wonderful to realize that when I don't demand that Carlin be or act a certain way in order to make me happy, I am actually given more than I ever thought I would get. When I feel from Carlin that it's okay to give only those things I genuinely feel like giving I'm amazed at how much love flows through me. Carlin sums up this process in the title of her book, *Love It, Don't Label It!*

Please remember that these statements concern our own experience thus far. They certainly don't represent the "truth" about healthy love or about addictive love. Each of us must find our own definitions of love. I encourage you to go inside yourself and see what truths emerge. Trust yourself. You can't make a mistake. Each experience will teach you more about love.

196

AFTERWORD

Before I became a writer I thought that authors were mythical creatures who didn't really exist. I would read words in a book that moved me or made a difference in my life, but never quite believed I could send my own thoughts to a real person.

I have tried to tell it from the heart. If you have been touched by anything in this book and would like to write to me, I would be pleased to hear from you. Truly, it is said that life is a dance we each do separately, together.

Jed Diamond, L.C.S.W.
P.O. Box 9355
San Rafael, CA 94912

AM I HOOKED OR AM I FREE?
A Self-Help Questionnaire

Author's Note: I generally dislike tests. They tend to label people as either "this" or "that" and contribute to the problem they are attempting to solve. Many times they are used by one person to try to get another person to change. Yet it can be very helpful to focus our attention on our attitudes and behavior so that we can decide for ourselves what changes, if any, need to be made in our lives.

I offer this test as a tool for you to better understand your own life. The questions are meant to shed light on your attitudes about your own romantic behavior.

The process of asking yourself these questions and wrestling with your own answers is much more important than your score. Let your answers be a guide toward understanding yourself better.

1. Do you keep secrets about your romantic activities from people who are important to you?

Never = 0   Seldom = 1   Sometimes = 2
Frequently = 3   Always = 4

2. Do you make love at inappropriate times, in inappropriate places, or with inappropriate people?

> Never = 0   Seldom = 1   Sometimes = 2
> Frequently = 3   Always = 4

3. Do you make promises to yourself or set rules for yourself concerning your romantic behavior that you find you don't follow?

> Never = 0   Seldom = 1   Sometimes = 2
> Frequently = 3   Always = 4

4. Do you feel uneasy when you are away from your lover?

> Never = 0   Seldom = 1   Sometimes = 2
> Frequently = 3   Always = 4

5. Do you engage in romantic activities regardless of the possible consequences (the threat of being caught, risk of contracting disease, personal danger, etc.)?

> Never = 0   Seldom = 1   Sometimes = 2
> Frequently = 3   Always = 4

6. Do you feel frustrated and angry if you don't get the kind of response to your romantic overtures that you expect?

> Never = 0   Seldom = 1   Sometimes = 2
> Frequently = 3   Always = 4

7. Do you have trouble leaving a relationship even when it becomes unsatisfying or destructive?

> Never = 0   Seldom = 1   Sometimes = 2
> Frequently = 3   Always = 4

8. Do your outside romantic activities threaten or damage a relationship that is important to you?

199

Never = 0   Seldom = 1   Sometimes = 2
Frequently = 3   Always = 4

9. Do you find yourself flirting with someone even if you don't mean to?

Never = 0   Seldom = 1   Sometimes = 2
Frequently = 3   Always = 4

10. Do you lose your sense of identity or the meaning of life without a love relationship?

Never = 0   Seldom = 1   Sometimes = 2
Frequently = 3   Always = 4

11. Do you make love or seek romantic involvements in order to try to deal with, or escape from, life's problems?

Never = 0   Seldom = 1   Sometimes = 2
Frequently = 3   Always = 4

12. Do you feel uncomfortable about your masturbation because of the frequency with which you masturbate, the fantasies you engage in, the props you use, and/or the places in which you do it?

Never = 0   Seldom = 1   Sometimes = 2
Frequently = 3   Always = 4

13. Do you find yourself needing greater and greater variety and novelty in your romantic activities just to achieve an acceptable level of physical and emotional relief?

Never = 0   Seldom = 1   Sometimes = 2
Frequently = 3   Always = 4

14. Do you feel afraid to get too close to people, concerned you may be hurt or abandoned?

200

Never = 0   Seldom = 1   Sometimes = 2
Frequently = 3   Always = 4

15. Do you obsess about sex or romance even when it interferes with your daily responsibilities or causes emotional discomfort?

    Never = 0   Seldom = 1   Sometimes = 2
    Frequently = 3   Always = 4

16. Do you wish you could stop or control your romantic activities?

    Never = 0   Seldom = 1   Sometimes = 2
    Frequently = 3   Always = 4

17. Do you feel you need romance in order to feel alive and whole?

    Never = 0   Seldom = 1   Sometimes = 2
    Frequently = 3   Always = 4

18. Do you feel that your romantic activities affect your spiritual life in a negative way?

    Never = 0   Seldom = 1   Sometimes = 2
    Frequently = 3   Always = 4

19. Do you think that there might be more you could do with your life if you were not so driven by romantic pursuits?

    Never = 0   Seldom = 1   Sometimes = 2
    Frequently = 3   Always = 4

20. Do you find yourself looking for romantic articles or scenes in newspapers, magazines, or other media?

    Never = 0   Seldom = 1   Sometimes = 2
    Frequently = 3   Always = 4

21. Do you feel remorse, shame, or guilt after a romantic encounter?

201

$$\text{Never} = 0 \quad \text{Seldom} = 1 \quad \text{Sometimes} = 2$$
$$\text{Frequently} = 3 \quad \text{Always} = 4$$

22. Does each new relationship continue to have the same destructive pattern as previous ones?

$$\text{Never} = 0 \quad \text{Seldom} = 1 \quad \text{Sometimes} = 2$$
$$\text{Frequently} = 3 \quad \text{Always} = 4$$

23. Do you think about avoiding intimate relationships because they are just too difficult or painful?

$$\text{Never} = 0 \quad \text{Seldom} = 1 \quad \text{Sometimes} = 2$$
$$\text{Frequently} = 3 \quad \text{Always} = 4$$

24. Does the time you spend reading romance novels or watching arousing films interfere with your daily activities or relationships with people?

$$\text{Never} = 0 \quad \text{Seldom} = 1 \quad \text{Sometimes} = 2$$
$$\text{Frequently} = 3 \quad \text{Always} = 4$$

25. Do you feel you are riding a crazy roller coaster of intense "highs" and crashing "lows"?

$$\text{Never} = 0 \quad \text{Seldom} = 1 \quad \text{Sometimes} = 2$$
$$\text{Frequently} = 3 \quad \text{Always} = 4$$

My total score is _____

How would you assess your current attitude toward love and romance?
( ) I'm having no problems
( ) I'm having minor problems
( ) I'm having moderate problems
( ) I'm having serious problems
( ) I'm a recovering love addict

Each person must make his or her own assessment of the answers to the questions and of how to interpret the score. However, if you find scores helpful, the following scores offer guidelines as to how other people taking the test have rated themselves:

No problems: 0 to 20
Minor problems: 21 to 30
Moderate problems: 31 to 60
Serious problems: 61 to 100

Recovering love addicts had various scores, depending on their stage of recovery.

Remember: These scores are meant to help you, not to pass some test. If you want to "prove" you are not having problems, you will see that you score below 20. If you are trying to convince yourself that you have serious problems, you will score above 61. Try to be as honest with yourself as possible.

Finally, if the test helps you, use it. If it hinders you, put it aside.

SOURCES FOR HELP

The following are national self-help programs dealing specifically with love addiction. Contact them if you wish to join a group in your area.

Augustine Fellowship, Sex and Love Addicts Anonymous. A 12-step fellowship based on AA for those who desire to stop living out a pattern of sex and love addiction, obsessive/compulsive sexual behavior or emotional attachment. Quarterly newsletter available. Write: P.O. Box 119, New Town Branch, Boston, MA 02258. Call (617) 332–1845.

S-Anon. A self-help program of recovery using the 12 Steps adapted from AA and Al-Anon, for those involved in relationships with people who have compulsive sexual behavior. Write: P.O. Box 5117, Sherman Oaks, California 91413.

NASAP (National Association on Sexual Addiction Problems). NASAP is a private, nonprofit organization established to promote public understanding, awareness, and recognition of sexual dependency problems by providing education, information, and referral services

204

throughout the professional and lay communities. Write: P.O. Box 696, Manhattan Beach, CA 90266. Call (213) 546–3101.

Sex Addicts Anonymous. Fellowship of men and women who share their experience, strength, and hope with one another that they may solve their common problem and gain freedom from compulsive sexual behavior. Guidelines available for starting new groups. Educational booklet also available. Write: P.O. Box 3038, Minneapolis, MN 55403. Call (612) 339–0217.

Sexaholics Anonymous. International program of recovery for those who want to stop sexually destructive thinking and behavior. Mutual support to achieve and maintain sexual sobriety. Phone network, newsletter, chapter development guidelines available. Write: P.O. Box 300, Simi Valley, CA 93062. Call (818) 704–9854.

The following are treatment centers around the U.S. dealing with the problems of love addiction.

ARIZONA
>   Sexual Recovery Program
>   333 W. Ft. Lowell #123
>   Tucson, AZ 85705
>   (602) 792–4792
>   Contact: Sherry Sedgwick, Director

CALIFORNIA
>   Center for Prospering Relationships
>   22 Salvador Way
>   San Rafael, CA 94903
>   (415) 472–4649
>   Contact: Jed Diamond, Director
>
>   Outpatient Services
>   1303 Avocado Ave. #230
>   Newport Beach, CA 92660
>   (714) 720–1250
>   Contact: David Lynn-Hill, Director
>
>   Rex Reece, Ph.D.
>   9229 Sunset Blvd. #608

West Hollywood, CA 90069
(213) 275–6546

Want Institute
3355 Via Lido #300
Newport Beach, CA 92663
(714) 673–WANT
Contact: Patricia D. Allen, Ph.D., Director

ILLINOIS

North Shore Counseling Inc.
946 Oak St.
Winnetka, IL 60093
(312) 446–8288
Contact: Mary Ann Miller, Director
Offices also in Northfield and Barrington/Crystal Lake area.

IOWA

Westside Clinical Associates
2600 72nd St., Suite D
Des Moines, IA 50311
(515) 270–1344
Contact: Dr. Anita Jordan, Director

KANSAS

Sexual Addictions Treatment Program
Prairie View, Inc.
Box 467
1901 East First St.
Newton, KS 67114
(316) 283–2400
Contact: Gerry Epp, M.S.W., A.C.S.W., Director

MICHIGAN

Children of Alcoholic Parents (CAPS)
4060 E. Twelve Mile Road
Warren, MI 48092
(313) 745–7464 or (313) 573–3125
Contact: Kenneth M. Adams, Ph.D., Director

Institute for Sex Therapy, Education and Research
420½ E. Front St.
Traverse City, MI 49684
(616) 947–2444
Contact: Barbara Jones Smith, Ph.D., Director

MINNESOTA

Alpha Human Services, Inc.
2712 Fremont Ave. South
Minneapolis, MN 55408
(612) 872–8218
Contact: Intake Director

Charlotte Eliza Kasl, Ph.D.
4134 Park Ave. South
Minneapolis, MN 55407
(612) 823–4143

Program in Human Sexuality
University of Minnesota Medical School
2630 University Ave. S.E.
Minneapolis, MN 55414
(612) 627–4360
Contact: Eli Coleman, Ph.D.

Ridgedale Counseling Service
12450 Wayzata Blvd., Suite 112
Minnetonka, MN 55343
(612) 542–8932
Contact: Del Kennedy, Director

Sexual Dependency Unit
Golden Valley Center
4101 Golden Valley Rd.
Golden Valley, MN 55422
(612) 588–2771
Contact: The Call Center

NEW JERSEY

In the Clearing

207

170 Bridge Ave.
Red Bank, NJ 07701
(201) 530–5344
Contact: Edwin E. Ellis, Ph.D.

NEW YORK

Counseling Resource Center
130 W. 44th St.
New York, NY 10036
(212) 382–2869
Contact: Harry Schaumburg, D.Min.

Sharon G. Nathan, Ph.D.
11 East 68th St.
New York, NY 10021
(212) 879–7610

NORTH CAROLINA

Barbara Kaplan, M.H.D.L.
501 Archdale Dr.
Charlotte, NC 28217
(704) 527–2108

OHIO

Tri-County Mental Health and Counseling Services, Inc.
28 West Stimson Ave.
Athens, OH 45701
(614) 592–3091
Contact: Michael Morrison, Director

OREGON

Chrysalis Counseling
P.O. Box 02336
Portland, OR 97202
(503) 775–4579
Contact: Lynn Carter

PENNSYLVANIA

Allied Counseling Services

1726 Pine St.
Philadelphia, PA
(215) 546–7688
Contact: William Lundgren, M.Ed., C.A.C.

Outpatient Addiction Treatment Services
111 N. 49th St.
Philadelphia, PA 19139
(215) 471–2491 .
Contact: Martha Turner, M.D.

TEXAS

SHARE (Sexuality, Human Awareness, and Relationship Education) Centers
3570 Vancouver
Dallas, TX 75229
(214) 357–2371
Contact: Rip Corley

WASHINGTON

Another Chance
Bellevue Community Services
1200 112th Ave. N.E.
Bellevue, WA 98004
(206) 454–0616
Contact: Dr. Bill Lennon

WYOMING

Geral Blanchard, A.C.P.S.
Cady Bldg., Suite 218
One East Alger
Sheridan, WY 82801
(306) 674–6309

For listings of other self-help programs in your area, call the following:

209

- Self-Help Clearinghouse, New Jersey (201) 625–7101. It publishes and updates *The Self-Help Sourcebook*, the most complete directory for finding and forming mutual-aid and self-help groups. It also can refer you to resources in Canada.
- Self-Help Center, Illinois (312) 328–0470
- National Self-Help Clearinghouse, New York City (212) 840–1259

NOTES

Introduction

1. *Love and Addiction*, New York, New American Library, 1975, p. 1. One of the first serious books on this subject, it is a classic and well worth reading.
2. These statistics are reported in an article in *American Medical News*, published June 5, 1987, by the American Medical Association. See also Dr. Carnes' *Out of the Shadows: Understanding Sexual Addiction*, Minneapolis, CompCare Publications, 1983. As the title suggests, Dr. Carnes brings sexual addiction out in the open. An excellent book.
3. The questions for the self-help questionnaire have been drawn from my own experience as well as from those of self-help groups: Sex and Love Addicts Anonymous, Sex Addicts Anonymous, and Sexaholics Anonymous.

Chapter 1

1. I first heard the phrase "compulsion, loss of control, and continued use in spite of the consequences" from Dr. David Smith, director of the Haight-Ashbury Free Medical Clinic.
2. *The Empty Fortress*, New York, The Free Press, 1967, p. 14.
3. Carol Pearson, *The Hero Within*. San Francisco: Harper & Row, 1986, pp. 27–32.
4. Warren Farrell, *Why Men Are the Way They Are*. New York: McGraw-Hill, 1986, pp. 58–59. This book has been the most valuable I've found for understanding men and women today.

5. Gerald Jampolsky, M.D., *Love Is Letting Go of Fear.* San Francisco: Celestial Arts, 1979.
6. Janice Keller Phelps, M.D., and Alan E. Nourse, M.D., *The Hidden Addictions and How to Get Free.* New York: Little, Brown & Company, 1986. Excellent book showing the relationship between alcoholism and other addictions, depression, and what we eat.
7. *Ceremonial Chemistry: The Ritual Persecution of Drugs, Addicts and Pushers,* New York, Anchor Press, 1974.
8. Jampolsky, op. cit., pp. 9–10.

Chapter 2

1. *Piece of My Heart,* New York, St. Martin's Press, 1971, p. 52. Dalton shows well the love addiction that drove Janis Joplin.
2. Ibid., p. 52.
3. Ibid., pp. 53–54.
4. Ibid., p. 86.
5. Ibid., p. 56.
6. The Augustine Fellowship, Sex and Love Addicts Anonymous. *Sex and Love Addicts Anonymous.* Boston: Fellowship-Wide Services, Inc., 1986. Excellent description of sex and love addictions through the words of the people who have lived through them.
7. *Out of the Shadows,* p. 136.
8. "Sexual Compulsivity: Definition, Etiology, and Treatment Considerations." *The Journal of Chemical Dependency Treatment,* Vol. 1, No. 1, 1987, pp. 189–204. Dr. Coleman is able to make sense out of a very confusing field.
9. *Love and Addiction,* pp. 1–12.
10. *When Society Becomes an Addict,* p. 18. San Francisco: Harper & Row, 1987. Dr. Schaef looks at addiction in a new way and shows how our whole society has become addictive. An excellent, innovative book.
11. *Fat Is a Family Affair.* San Francisco: Harper & Row, 1985, p. xii. An excellent book that shows the relationship between love addiction and food addiction.
12. Charles L. Whitfield, M.D., *Healing The Child Within: Discovery and Recovery for Adult Children of Dysfunctional Families.* Pompano Beach, Florida: Health Communications, 1987. This book describes the journey to finding the real self in clinically-orientated yet readable fashion.
13. *Wealth Addiction.* New York: E. P. Dutton, 1983. A little-known book that sheds real light on our preoccupation with money and our addictive society.

Chapter 4

1. There has been a great deal written about the role of the family in understanding addictions. I have found the following works particularly valuable: Melody Beattie's *Codependent No More: How to Stop Controlling Others and Start Caring for Yourself,* Elizabeth Janeway's *Man's World, Woman's Place,* Anne Wilson Schaef's *Co-Dependence: Misunderstood, Mistreated,* and Sharon Wegscheider's *Another Chance: Hope & Health for the Alcoholic Family.*

2. Dr. Farrell has developed these ideas over many years working with more than 100,000 men and women in group situations.

3. *The Other Side of the Coin: Causes and Consequences of Men's Oppression.* Madison, Wisconsin: Bioenergetics Press, 1982, p. 72. This book has not gotten the attention it deserves.

4. See, for instance, Connell O'Brien Cowan & Melvyn Kinder, *Smart Women, Foolish Choices;* Colette Dowling, *The Cinderella Complex;* Susan Forward and Joan Torres, *Men Who Hate Women & The Women Who Love Them;* Robin Norwood, *Women Who Love Too Much;* and Natalie Shainess, M.D., *Sweet Suffering.* I prefer Robin Norwood's book for its combination of personal experience and clinical insight.

5. See Robin Norwood's *Women Who Love Too Much* for a good description of love addiction in women.

6. See Judy Allen, *Picking on Men.* New York: Ballantine Books, 1986. This compilation of male put-downs helps us understand why so many men feel bad about themselves.

7. See Ann Neitlich, *Building Bridges: Women's & Men's Liberation.* Building Bridges, P.O. Box 461, Cambridge, MA 02140, 1985. An excellent description of the ways in which both men and women are victims of conditioning. The most balanced liberation book I've read.

8. See Elizabeth Janeway, *Man's World, Woman's Place,* New York, Dell Publishing Co., 1971; and Lillian B. Rubin, *Intimate Strangers,* New York: Harper & Row, 1983. These books are gems. I highly recommend them to those who want to understand men and women without looking to blame one group or the other.

9. See Samuel Osherson, *Finding Our Fathers.* New York: The Free Press, 1986. A good description of the importance of fathers in the lives of both men and women.

10. See Gayle Kimball, *50–50 Parenting.* Lexington, MA: Lexington Books, 1987. Dr. Kimball suggests that equal parenting can be a key to liberation for both men and women.

11. See Dorothy Dinnerstein, *The Mermaid and the Minotaur.* New York:

Harper & Row, 1976. Dinnerstein's ideas on the ways in which males and females are conditioned are quite profound.

12. Beverly V. Romberger, in "Commonplaces Women Learned About Relating to Men." *American Behavioral Scientist*, January/February, 1986, pp. 342–367.
13. See Pierre Mornell, M.D., *Passive Men, Wild Women*. New York: Ballantine Books, 1979.

Chapter 5

1. *Psychology of Science*. New York, Harper & Row, 1966. Maslow's work on basic needs gives us a real understanding of what is necessary for human health and well-being.
2. *Childhood and Society*. New York: W. W. Norton, 1963.
3. Ibid., p. 249.
4. See M. Scott Peck, *The Road Less Traveled: The Psychology of Spiritual Growth*. New York: Simon & Schuster, 1978. Peck also makes the connection between the loss of basic trust and the spiritual vulnerability experienced by addicts. In a 1987 lecture in Berkeley, California, he called addiction "the sacred disease."
5. See Howard Halpern, *How to Break Your Addiction to a Person*. New York: McGraw-Hill, 1982. Halpern describes well the addict's terror at losing his or her love object.

Chapter 6

1. See Stephanie Brown, *Treating the Alcoholic*. New York: John Wiley & Sons, 1985. An excellent book on understanding and treating alcoholism. The insights can be applied to all addictions.

Chapter 7

1. See Ernest Kurtz, *Shame and Guilt: Characteristics of the Dependency Cycle*. Minneapolis: Hazelden, 1981. Kurtz, author of the excellent book on the history of AA, *Not-God*, gives a good description of the way in which guilt and shame are experienced by the addict.
2. *Fathers and Daughers*. New York: Berkley Books, 1981. Excellent book on the stages of the father-daughter relationship.

Chapter 8

1. *Love and Limerence: The Experience of Being in Love*. New York: Stein and Day, 1979, pp. vii, viii. A classic book that will tell you more about love than you might want to know.

214

2. Since all the 12-step programs are based on the pioneering work of Alcoholics Anonymous, I highly recommend that those interested in recovery read *Alcoholics Anonymous*, the basic text for members of AA. I also believe that anyone interested in recovery from any addiction should attend a number of AA meetings.

Chapter 9
1. *The End of Sex: Erotic Love After the Sexual Revolution.* Los Angeles: Jeremy P. Tarcher, 1983. One of the best books on sex and love I have read.
2. Helen & Stan Dale, Sex Workshops for 1988, 2814 San Carlos Ave., San Carlos, CA 94070; (415) 593–2612. There are many workshops on "sex and love." I think Helen and Stan's are among the very best.

BIBLIOGRAPHY

Alcoholics Anonymous World Services. *Alcoholics Anonymous*. New York: Alcoholics Anonymous World Services, Inc., 1976.

Allen, Judy. *Picking on Men*. New York: Ballantine Books, 1986.

Appleton, William, M.D. *Fathers and Daughters*. New York: Berkley Books, 1981.

The Augustine Fellowship, Sex and Love Addicts Anonymous. *Sex and Love Addicts Anonymous*. Boston: Fellowship-Wide Services, Inc., 1986.

Beattie, Melody. *Codependent No More: How to Stop Controlling Others and Start Caring for Yourself*. San Francisco: Harper & Row, 1987.

Bettelheim, Bruno. *The Empty Fortress*. New York: The Free Press, 1967.

Brown, Stephanie. *Treating the Alcoholic*. New York: John Wiley & Sons, 1985.

Carnes, Patrick J. *Out of the Shadows: Understanding Sexual Addiction*. Minneapolis: CompCare Publications, 1983.

Coleman, Eli. "Sexual Compulsivity: Definition, Etiology, and Treatment Considerations." *The Journal of Chemical Dependency Treatment*, Vol. 1, No. 1, 1987.

CompCare Publishers. *Hope & Recovery: A Twelve-Step Guide for Healing from Compulsive Sexual Behavior*. Minneapolis: CompCare Publishers, 1987.

216

Cowan, Connell O'Brien and Melvyn Kinder. *Smart Women, Foolish Choices.* New York: Clarkson N. Potter, 1985.

Dalton, David. *Piece of My Heart.* New York: St. Martin's Press, 1971.

Diamond, Carlin. *Love It, Don't Label It! A Practical Guide for Using Spiritual Principles in Everyday Life.* San Rafael, CA: Fifth Wave Press, 1985.

Diamond, Jed. *Inside Out: Becoming My Own Man.* San Rafael, CA: Fifth Wave Press, 1983.

Dinnerstein, Dorothy. *The Mermaid and the Minotaur.* New York: Harper & Row, 1976.

Dowling, Colette. *The Cinderella Complex.* New York: Pocket Books, 1981.

Erikson, Erik H. *Childhood and Society.* New York: W. W. Norton, 1963.

Farrell, Warren. *Why Men Are the Way They Are.* New York: McGraw-Hill, 1986.

Forward, Susan and Joan Torres. *Men Who Hate Women & The Women Who Love Them.* New York: Bantam Books, 1986.

Greenfield, Sidney M. "Love and Marriage in Modern America: A Functional Analysis." *The Sociological Quarterly*, No. 6, 1965.

Halpern, Howard. *How to Break Your Addiction to a Person.* New York: McGraw-Hill, 1982.

Hollis, Judi. *Fat Is a Family Affair.* San Francisco: Harper & Row, 1985.

Jampolsky, Gerald, M.D. *Love Is Letting Go of Fear.* San Francisco: Celestial Arts, 1979.

Janeway, Elizabeth. *Man's World, Woman's Place.* New York: Dell Publishing Co., 1971.

Johnson, Vernon E. *I'll Quit Tomorrow.* New York: Harper & Row, 1980.

Jung, C. G. *Memories, Dreams, Reflections.* Recorded and edited by Aniela Jaffé. New York: Vantage Books, 1961.

Kasl, Charlotte. *Women and Sex Addiction.* Minneapolis: Castle Consulting, Inc., 1984.

Kiley, Dan. *The Wendy Dilemma.* New York: Avon Books, 1984.

Kimball, Gayle. *50–50 Parenting.* Lexington, MA: Lexington Books, 1987.

Kurtz, Ernest. *Not-God: A History of Alcoholics Anonymous.* Minneapolis: Hazelden, 1979.

———. *Shame and Guilt: Characteristics of the Dependency Cycle.* Minneapolis: Hazelden, 1981.

Larsen, Earnie. *Stage II Recovery: Life Beyond Addiction.* New York: Harper & Row, 1985.

Leonard, George. *The End of Sex: Erotic Love After the Sexual Revolution.* Los Angeles: Jeremy P. Tarcher, 1983.

217

Luthman, Shirley Gehrke. *Collection 1979.* San Rafael, CA: Mehetabel & Company, 1980.

Maslow, Abraham. *Psychology of Science.* New York: Harper & Row, 1966.

Mead, Margaret. *Male and Female.* New York: William Morrow, 1949.

Milkman, Harvey B. and Howard J. Shaffer. *The Addictions.* Lexington, MA: D. C. Heath & Company, 1985.

Mornell, Pierre, M.D. *Passive Men, Wild Women.* New York: Ballantine Books, 1979.

Neitlich, Ann. *Building Bridges: Women's & Men's Liberation.* Building Bridges, P.O. Box 461, Cambridge, MA 02140, 1985.

Norwood, Robin. *Women Who Love Too Much.* New York: Pocket Books, 1985.

Osherson, Samuel. *Finding Our Fathers.* New York: The Free Press, 1986.

Pearson, Carol. *The Hero Within.* San Francisco: Harper & Row, 1986.

Peck, M. Scott. *The Road Less Traveled: The Psychology of Spiritual Growth.* New York: Simon & Schuster, 1978.

Peele, Stanton. *Love and Addiction.* New York: New American Library, 1975.

Phelps, Janice Keller, M.D., and Alan E. Nourse, M.D. *The Hidden Addictions and How to Get Free.* New York: Little, Brown & Company, 1986.

Rubin, Lillian B. *Intimate Strangers.* New York: Harper & Row, 1983.

Schaef, Anne Wilson. *Co-Dependence: Misunderstood, Mistreated.* Minneapolis: Winston Press, 1986.

———. *When Society Becomes an Addict.* San Francisco: Harper & Row, 1987.

Schenk, Roy. *The Other Side of the Coin: Causes and Consequences of Men's Oppression.* Madison, Wisconsin: Bioenergetics Press, 1982.

Seymour, Richard B. and David E. Smith, M.D. *DrugFree: A Unique, Positive Approach to Staying Off Alcohol and Other Drugs.* New York: Sarah Lazin Books, 1987.

Shainess, Natalie, M.D. *Sweet Suffering.* New York: Pocket Books, 1984.

Slater, Phillip. *Wealth Addiction.* New York: E. P. Dutton, 1983.

Szasz, Thomas. *Ceremonial Chemistry: The Ritual Persecution of Drugs, Addicts and Pushers.* New York: Anchor Press, 1974.

Tennov, Dorothy. *Love and Limerence: The Experience of Being in Love.* New York: Stein and Day, 1979.

Time Magazine. "Back Off, Buddy: A new Hite report stirs up a furor over sex and love in the 80's." October 12, 1987.

Vaillant, George E. *The Natural History of Alcoholism: Causes, Patterns, and*

Paths to Recovery. Cambridge, MA: Harvard University Press, 1983.

Wegscheider, Sharon. *Another Chance: Hope & Health for the Alcoholic Family*. Palo Alto: Science and Behavior Books, 1981.

Weil, Andrew, M.D. and Winifred Rosen. *Chocolate to Morphine: Understanding Mind-Active Drugs*. Boston: Houghton Mifflin Company, 1983.

Welwood, John, editor. *Challenge of the Heart*. Boston: Shambhala Publications, 1985.

Zinberg, Norman, M.D. *Drug, Set, and Setting: The Basis for Controlled Intoxicant Use*. New Haven: Yale University Press, 1984.

INDEX